FEDS VS YOU

SENTENCE REDUCTION EDITION

PATRICK HALL SR.

Disclaimer

The information provided in this book is not intended as, and should not be construed as, legal advice. The author, Patrick Hall, is not a licensed attorney, and the content of this book should not be used as a substitute for professional legal counsel. While every effort has been made to provide accurate and up-to-date information, laws, legal procedures, and their interpretation can change frequently, and each case is unique.

For specific legal advice or representation, you should seek the assistance of a qualified attorney who can provide personalized guidance based on the facts and circumstances of your case.

The author and publisher disclaim any liability for any losses or damages arising from the use of this book's content. By reading this book, you acknowledge and agree that the author and publisher are not liable for any actions or decisions you may take based on the information presented.

TABLE OF CONTENTS

“The Path to a Lighter Sentence: Strategies for Securing a Downward Departure”

Understanding the Foundations of Downward Departures

INTRODUCTION

When a person is sentenced, the focus often shifts solely to the crime they committed, with little regard for the complex, multifaceted factors that contributed to their actions. But behind every case is a human being, with their own story, struggles, and hopes for redemption. A sentence is not just a punishment; it is an event that ripples out, affecting not only the individual but also their family, their community, and their future. Every person deserves the chance to make things right and return to the ones they love, to rebuild their life, and to contribute positively to society. This is why understanding how the law allows for downward departures is crucial—because it isn't just about the reduction of time served; it's about providing a person with the opportunity to reclaim their life and return to the people who need them most.

Each part of this guide explores the powerful factors that can influence a sentence—factors that consider not just the crime, but the person behind it. Cooperation with authorities, mental capacity, family responsibilities, remorse, health issues, and the involvement of others in the crime all play a role in determining the outcome of a case. These considerations can lead to a more compassionate sentence, one that acknowledges the potential for growth and redemption.

It's important to remember that our journey isn't defined by a single mistake. The opportunity for a second chance is not just an abstract notion—it's a tangible, life-changing possibility. For many, the drive to return home to family can be the spark that ignites a commitment to change. In this guide, we'll explore how each of these factors can be used to advocate for a downward departure, ultimately helping to bring you back home, where you belong, to continue your journey of healing and transformation. Your family is waiting, and this is the first step toward ensuring you have the chance to go back to them.

CHAPTER 1

Substantial Assistance to Authorities (5K1.1)

Cooperation with law enforcement is not an easy decision. It's a path fraught with risk, sacrifice, and uncertainty. Yet, for those who find themselves caught in the web of the justice system, offering substantial assistance to authorities can be the most powerful tool to reduce a sentence. It's a choice that forces an individual to step out of the shadows of their past and into the light of accountability, a willingness to work alongside the very forces they once feared.

When someone agrees to cooperate with law enforcement, it's more than just a simple act of providing information. It's about providing critical intelligence that can dismantle criminal organizations, track down key figures, and unravel the complex web of illegal activity. The stakes are high. For some, cooperating means putting their safety on the line, not only by risking their freedom but by exposing themselves to potential retaliation from criminal associates. Yet, this cooperation is viewed by the courts as a tangible act of redemption.

This process isn't always about a personal desire for leniency; sometimes, it's about realizing that their actions, as harmful as they were, can also serve as the key to bringing down larger operations and preventing future crimes. In essence, cooperating with law enforcement offers a dual opportunity: the chance for the individual to atone for their own role in the criminal world, and the chance for law enforcement to protect society at large. By exposing the deeper layers of criminal activity, a defendant who cooperates becomes part of a larger picture—one where their actions can potentially save lives, dismantle dangerous networks, and lead to justice in a broader sense.

However, the decision to assist is never made lightly. There is a deeply human struggle in turning over information that could implicate others. It's a fight between loyalty to old associations and the weight of knowing that helping law enforcement could be a path to personal redemption. For many, it's an emotional and mental battle, torn between the loyalty to their past and the desire to create a better future. The fear of consequences—be it from the criminal underworld or from the societal judgment they know they'll face—can be overwhelming.

But when the court sees genuine cooperation—when they witness someone who has helped to bring down networks and provided invaluable insight—they recognize it as a powerful act of personal transformation. The individual who once engaged in illegal activities and helped perpetuate harm is now working to stop that same harm. In the eyes of the court, this transformation can mean everything. Cooperation is not merely about compliance—it's a sign of someone who has stepped into their own accountability, who is willing to face the consequences not only for their own actions but for the greater good.

This is why a downward departure under 5K1.1, the substantial assistance to authorities provision, can be so significant. The law recognizes that people can change. They can become more than their crimes. By assisting law enforcement, a person proves that they are no longer simply a part of the problem, but instead, they have become part of the solution. It's an acknowledgment that, even after a life of crime, there is still a chance for a person to prove their value, to show that they are capable of helping to make the world safer.

In the end, substantial assistance isn't just about reducing a sentence—it's about redemption. It's the chance to demonstrate that no matter how far one has fallen, they still have the ability to rise, to contribute, and to change the trajectory of their own life. It is an opportunity to leave behind the darkness and step into the possibility of a new chapter, one where the individual can show their worth not by the crimes they committed, but by the good they chose to do after the fact.

CHAPTER 2

Understanding the Foundations of Downward Departures Criminal History (4A1.3)

The weight of the past often hangs over us like a shadow, casting its darkness on everything we try to build in the present. When it comes to sentencing, a criminal history is often treated as a permanent marker, a stain that cannot be erased, no matter the efforts we make to change. Yet, in some cases, that history is not a fair reflection of who we are today. Sometimes, the story behind an individual's past is far more complex than what a criminal record shows. And it is in these moments that the possibility of a downward departure due to criminal history becomes a beacon of hope.

A criminal history does more than just represent past wrongdoings—it is used to forecast the future. A judge, when determining the severity of a sentence, may lean heavily on the history of the defendant, assuming that a pattern of crime is likely to continue. This reliance on the past can create an unfair picture, one that fails to take into account the growth, change, and personal transformation that may have occurred since those earlier convictions. For those who have truly worked to move beyond their mistakes, an overrepresentation of their criminal history can feel like a constant reminder of a life they no longer live.

The idea of overrepresentation in criminal history is powerful because it acknowledges that Sometimes, a defendant's past doesn't define their present. A person who has committed offenses in their younger years, who may have acted out of desperation or circumstances beyond their control, should not necessarily be judged as the same person in their later years. Over time, a person can mature, learn from their mistakes, and make efforts to turn their life around. For those who have made significant strides to rehabilitate themselves—through education, therapy, or simply a commitment to leading a law-abiding life—their criminal history might no longer reflect the person they've become.

Consider the individual who, in their youth, was caught up in a cycle of crime, perhaps influenced by their environment or driven by external pressures. Over time, however, they may have found the strength to break free from those circumstances. They may have found stability through employment, family, or a commitment to community. But the criminal record they carry still reflects those earlier years, the mistakes that they wish they could erase but cannot. This is where a downward departure for criminal history can play a pivotal role.

The sentencing guidelines recognize that not all criminal histories are equally relevant. For example, a conviction from a distant past, particularly one that doesn't reflect current behavior, may not accurately predict the future actions of an individual. In these cases, a judge may consider whether the defendant's criminal history has been overly relied upon and whether it's skewing the fairness of the sentence. If a person's past crimes were committed during a time when they were young and reckless, or if those offenses are unrelated to the current charge, it may be fair to argue that the criminal history is not an accurate gauge of who the person is today.

For individuals who have shown they are capable of change, the law offers an opportunity to argue that their criminal history should not be weighed so heavily in sentencing. The focus shifts from the past to the present: Have they demonstrated a commitment to change? Have they distanced themselves from the behaviors that once defined them? This focus on personal growth and transformation is crucial. A history that once seemed indicative of a dangerous pattern of behavior may, in fact, be an outdated relic that fails to reflect the person standing before the court today.

In these cases, a downward departure based on criminal history isn't about excusing past actions; it's about fairness. It's about ensuring that an individual's sentence isn't inflated due to a history that no longer accurately represents their current state. This departure recognizes that people can and do change, and that the focus of the justice system should be on how a person is now, not just how they were in the past.

The emotional weight of this process is significant. For those who have worked tirelessly to rebuild their lives, a sentence that punishes them for past mistakes can feel like a second sentence—one that traps them in the identity of who they once were, not who they've become. But with the argument for downward departure, there is the chance for a more nuanced view, one that reflects the person's present reality and acknowledges the efforts they've made to move forward. It is an opportunity to have the past acknowledged for what it was but not allowed to dictate the future.

The chance for a downward departure due to criminal history is a chance for justice to reflect more than just the crimes committed. It's a chance for the court to recognize that the individual before them is not the same person as the one who made mistakes years ago. It's a moment to allow the possibility of redemption to shine through, offering a sentence that reflects the individual's true potential and the person they are today—not simply the actions they took in a distant past. And for those who have worked hard to make amends and become better, this departure can be the opening of a new chapter—one that holds hope, possibility, and a future shaped by the lessons learned from their past.

CHAPTER 3

Diminished Capacity (5K2.13)

There is a profound and often overlooked reality within the justice system—one that goes beyond crime and punishment, beyond right and wrong. It is the reality of the human mind, the struggles that many face but few understand. When a person commits a crime while suffering from diminished capacity due to mental health issues, the question of accountability becomes more complex. This is not about excusing actions but about recognizing that not everyone who stands before the court arrived there under the same circumstances.

Diminished capacity is not a loophole; it is a plea for understanding. It acknowledges that some individuals, at the time of their offense, were not thinking rationally, not fully in control of their decisions, and not operating with the same mental clarity as others. Mental health struggles—whether caused by trauma, illness, or cognitive impairments—can cloud judgment, warp perception, and push individuals into actions they may not have taken had they been of sound mind. And yet, the justice system, built on the principles of responsibility and punishment, often struggles with how to address these realities.

A person suffering from severe depression, schizophrenia, PTSD, or another mental health disorder may not have intended to harm anyone. They may have been acting out of fear, paranoia, or a complete detachment from reality. Their actions might not reflect who they are at their core, but rather the symptoms of an illness that consumed them at the time. The courts recognize this in limited ways, offering a downward departure under

5K2.13 for those whose mental capacity was significantly impaired at the time of their offense. This does not mean absolution—it means fairness.

Imagine a man who has battled untreated PTSD for years, his mind replaying horrors from his past like a film on an endless loop. He turns to self-medication, numbing his pain in the only way he knows how. One night, in the depths of his mental suffering, he makes a terrible decision—a crime he would have never committed had his mind been clear. Does he deserve to be held accountable? Yes. But does he deserve to be sentenced as if he were of the same state of mind as someone who acted with full intent and awareness? No.

This is the distinction that diminished capacity seeks to make. It recognizes that while a person may have committed an offense, the extent of their culpability is influenced by the state of their mind at that moment. It does not dismiss responsibility, but it does demand a more nuanced approach to justice—one that sees the human being behind the act, one that understands the role of mental illness in shaping decisions, and one that refuses to treat all offenders as if they are the same.

Proving diminished capacity is not easy. It requires expert testimony, psychological evaluations, and a willingness from the court to consider the complexities of mental health. But for those who qualify, a downward departure can mean the difference between a sentence that destroys their future and one that allows them the chance to heal and rebuild. It can mean receiving treatment instead of simply being locked away. It can mean an acknowledgment from the system that justice is not just about punishment—it is about understanding, rehabilitation, and fairness.

There is still stigma surrounding mental illness in the legal system, and many defendants fear that bringing up their struggles will be seen as weakness or manipulation. But the reality is that mental health cannot be ignored. The law provides this downward departure because it recognizes the truth: mental illness affects behavior. It affects decision-making. It alters the way a person experiences the world. And when that illness plays a role in a crime, it should be considered in sentencing.

A sentence should reflect not only what a person has done but who they are and what led them to that moment. For those suffering from diminished capacity, a downward departure is more than just a legal argument—it is a plea for the justice system to recognize their humanity. It is a chance for the court to acknowledge that some people need help more than they need punishment. And for those fighting for a second chance, it is a small but powerful step toward a future where their illness does not define them—where they are seen not just for their worst moment but for their potential to rise above it.

CHAPTER 4

Aberrant Behavior (5K2.20)

There are moments in life that define us—times when we stand at a crossroads, making decisions that shape the way we are seen by the world. But what happens when a single moment, one lapse in judgment, one mistake, threatens to erase a lifetime of good character? For those who have lived their lives as law-abiding citizens, a single act of wrongdoing can feel like a devastating stain on everything they've worked for. The law recognizes this reality through the downward departure for aberrant behavior under 5K2.20, offering a chance for fairness when an offense is truly an isolated event.

Aberrant behavior means an act so out of character that it does not align with a person's past. It is the mistake of someone who has never been in trouble before, someone who—by all accounts—is not a criminal but a person who made a single, uncharacteristic misstep. This departure is a recognition that people are more than their worst moment. It acknowledges that human beings, no matter how responsible, are capable of error.

Imagine a man who has spent his life working hard, taking care of his family, and doing everything by the book. He has never been arrested, never been in trouble. But one day, in a moment of desperation, fear, or pressure, he makes a decision he immediately regrets. Perhaps it was financial strain that led him to commit fraud. Perhaps it was a trusted friend who convinced him to make a choice he wouldn't have considered under normal circumstances. Regardless of the specifics, the key is that this was not who he is—this was an exception, not a pattern.

The justice system Is often rigid, viewing crime through a lens of punishment rather than understanding. But this departure serves as a recognition that not all crimes are committed by career criminals. Some offenses are the result of temporary lapses in judgment, emotional distress, or even sheer panic. They are not a reflection of a person's true nature, and they are unlikely to be repeated.

To qualify for a downward departure based on aberrant behavior, a defendant must demonstrate that their crime was truly an isolated incident. The court will consider factors such as the individual's criminal history—or lack thereof—the circumstances of the offense, and whether the act appears to be part of a broader pattern. If the person has lived an otherwise honest and upstanding life, the argument can be made that their crime was an exception rather than the rule.

This departure is not for those who have repeatedly broken the law. It is not for those with a history of criminal conduct. It is for those who, if not for this single event, would never have found themselves in a courtroom at all. The law acknowledges that people make mistakes, and that one misstep should not define an entire lifetime of good deeds.

For many, seeking this departure is about more than reducing a sentence—it is about fighting for their identity. It is about proving to the court, to their loved ones, and to themselves that they are not the crime they committed. They are more than this one moment. They are the sum of all the choices they've made before and after.

Regret weighs heavily on those who have made a single, life-altering mistake. The guilt, the shame, the fear of being forever judged by one action—it can be overwhelming. But this departure offers a light in the darkness, a chance to be seen for who they truly are rather than who they were in their worst moment. It is a reminder that the justice system, at its best, is not just about punishment—it is about recognizing humanity, redemption, and the reality that one mistake should not erase a lifetime of integrity.

CHAPTER 5

Post-Offense Rehabilitation (5K2.19)

Redemption is not found in words alone—it is proven through action, through the difficult and deliberate steps a person takes to rebuild after a mistake. When someone stands before a judge, they are not only being sentenced for their crime; they are being judged for who they are in that moment. Are they the same person who committed the offense, or have they taken real steps to change? The law recognizes this transformation through a downward departure for post-offense rehabilitation under 5K2.19. It is a chance to show the court that a person is not defined by their past but by the effort they make to create a better future.

Rehabilitation is not about avoiding consequences—it is about proving that punishment alone is not what ensures justice. True justice considers growth. The courts understand that some individuals, after committing a crime, make an extraordinary effort to turn their lives around. They take accountability, they change their behavior, and they make amends—not because they are forced to, but because they genuinely want to be better. This is the essence of post-offense rehabilitation: demonstrating to the court that incarceration is not the only—or even the best—way to ensure a person does not re-offend.

Imagine a man who made a terrible mistake, one that cost him his freedom and his reputation. He could have let that mistake define him, allowing shame and bitterness to consume him. Instead, he chose to rebuild. While waiting for sentencing, he pursued education, sought counseling, entered drug treatment, or dedicated himself to community service. He repaired relationships, found faith, or mentored others to keep them from making the same mistakes. He did not do these things for the court—he did them for himself, because he knew that his actions, not his words, were the only proof of his transformation.

The courts do not take post-offense rehabilitation lightly. It is not enough to simply say, "I have changed." A person must show that change through consistent, meaningful effort. Have they taken responsibility for their actions? Have they sought help for underlying issues such as addiction, anger, or poor decision-making? Have they contributed positively to their community? Judges are not easily swayed by empty gestures—they want to see evidence that an individual has done the hard work to ensure they never stand before the court again.

The legal system often focuses on punishment as a means of deterrence, but true deterrence comes from personal growth. A person who has taken the initiative to better themselves is far less likely to reoffend than someone who is simply afraid of another prison sentence. Rehabilitation proves that incarceration is not the only way to achieve justice—sometimes, a person who has actively transformed their life does not need more punishment. They need a chance to move forward.

Post-offense rehabilitation is not about avoiding accountability. It is about proving that accountability has already taken place. It is about showing the court that the person standing before them today is not the same person who committed the crime. It is a powerful argument for mercy, not because the individual is asking for leniency, but because they have already done the work to earn it.

For those seeking this downward departure, the key is sincerity. Judges have seen every excuse, every fake promise of change. They are not looking for words—they are looking for proof. Rehabilitation is not a performance; it is a commitment. And for those who have truly embraced that commitment, this departure offers something greater than a reduced sentence. It offers recognition that people can change, that mistakes do not have to define a person's future, and that justice, when applied correctly, can be about more than just punishment—it can be about redemption.

The Power of Redemption: How Significant Positive Change After an Offense Can Impact Your Sentence

A single moment can alter the course of a life forever. A poor decision, a lapse in judgment, a mistake made in desperation—these things can define a person in the eyes of the law. But what if that moment, that mistake, was only a chapter and not the whole story? What if, in the aftermath of a crime, a person takes it upon themselves to change, to grow, to become someone unrecognizable from the person who once stood at the crossroads of right and wrong? The legal system, though often rigid, acknowledges that change is possible. Significant positive change after an offense can mean the difference between a harsh sentence and a second chance.

The weight of a conviction is heavy, pressing down on a person's identity, their future, and their sense of self-worth. In the beginning, it may feel like the walls are closing in, like the label of "criminal" is permanent. But change is a choice—a difficult one, a painful one, but a choice nonetheless. The courts know that rehabilitation is real when it is backed by action. A person who takes steps to better themselves—whether through education, therapy, community service, or personal growth—is proving something crucial: they are not the same person who committed the crime.

Judges and prosecutors are not just looking at the crime itself; they are looking at the individual standing before them. Have they made excuses, or have they taken accountability? Have they remained stagnant, or have they made an effort to rebuild? A man who, after his offense, earns his GED, mentors young people, seeks counseling, or works to repair relationships is showing the court something powerful. He is showing that he understands the depth of his mistake and is doing everything in his power to make sure he never returns to this place again.

It is easy to say, "I'm sorry." It is much harder to prove it through action. The justice system, despite its flaws, recognizes true rehabilitation. A person who has demonstrated consistent, meaningful change is a person who does not need to be broken further by a long, harsh sentence. A person who has faced their mistakes head-on and chosen growth is not the same person who committed the crime in the first place.

The impact of positive change on sentencing is not just about leniency—it is about justice. True justice is not just about punishment; it is about understanding who a person is at the time of sentencing, not just who they were at the time of their crime. When a person stands before a judge and can prove that they have worked tirelessly to rebuild, to learn, to make amends, that judge has the discretion to see them for who they are now, not who they were then.

This journey is not easy. The road to redemption is long, often filled with doubt, setbacks, and the weight of past choices. But for those who commit to it fully, who embrace change with sincerity and dedication, the law provides an opportunity for recognition. A reduced sentence is not a gift—it is an acknowledgment that people can grow, that mistakes do not have to define a lifetime, and that sometimes, the most just decision is to give a person the chance to continue on the path they have already begun.

Part 2

Leveraging Personal Circumstances for a Reduced Sentence

CHAPTER 6

Family Ties and Responsibilities (5H1.6)

When a person stands before the court, awaiting judgment, the focus is often solely on the crime committed. But beyond the charges, beyond the defendant's own actions, there exists a reality that the justice system sometimes overlooks: the people who depend on them. A sentence does not just punish the individual—it punishes their family. It is for this reason that the law allows for a downward departure based on family ties and responsibilities under 5H1.6.

Family is more than just a word—it is a bond, a responsibility, a commitment. A father who tucks his child in at night, a daughter who cares for an aging parent, a husband who supports his wife through illness—these are the roles that define a person's place in the world. When a defendant has deep, irreplaceable family obligations, removing them from their home does more than fulfill a legal penalty; it creates a ripple effect of suffering that extends far beyond the courtroom.

The courts recognize that some individuals are the sole providers for their families. They are the ones who put food on the table, who ensure their children have a roof over their heads, who care for disabled relatives who have no one else. In these cases, sending them away for an extended period is not just a punishment—it is a sentence imposed on their loved ones as well.

Judges consider several factors when evaluating whether family responsibilities warrant a downward departure. Is the defendant the primary caregiver for a child, a parent, or a spouse? Will their absence create an undue hardship that cannot be remedied by someone else stepping in? Have they been actively involved in their family's lives, demonstrating a pattern of love, responsibility, and care? The argument must be clear: the harm of removing this person from their family outweighs the benefit of a longer sentence.

Consider a single mother who made a mistake—perhaps a financial crime out of desperation—but who is the only person responsible for raising her children. If she is taken away, who will care for them? Will they be placed into a system that could change the course of their lives for the worse? The court must weigh whether justice is truly served by imposing a harsh sentence or whether an alternative punishment—one that allows her to continue providing for her family—better serves the interests of society.

Or imagine a son who has been the sole caregiver for his elderly, disabled father. If he is incarcerated, there is no one else to take on that burden. His father will suffer, potentially losing the ability to live with dignity. The court has the discretion to recognize that, in such cases, leniency is not just compassion—it is fairness.

Family obligations do not erase wrongdoing, nor do they absolve a person of responsibility. But they do matter. They are a reflection of a person's character, their role in the world outside of the crime they committed. A sentence should not destroy families when alternatives exist that still hold a person accountable while allowing them to fulfill their vital responsibilities.

For those seeking this downward departure, the key is proof. Letters from family members, testimony from those who rely on them, and evidence of their essential role in their household can make a difference. Judges do not want empty pleas for mercy—they want to see the undeniable truth that a severe sentence would create unnecessary suffering for innocent people.

Justice is not meant to be blind to humanity. A person is more than their crime—they are a parent, a child, a spouse, a provider. The law acknowledges that in some cases, the greater injustice would be separating them from those who need them most. A downward departure for family ties and responsibilities is not a loophole—it is a recognition that punishment should not come at the cost of destroying lives beyond the defendant's own.

CHAPTER 7

Age (5H1.1)

The weight of a sentence is not felt the same by all. A young person, barely stepping into adulthood, may carry the burden of their mistakes differently than an elderly individual whose remaining years are few. The law acknowledges this truth through 5H1.1, recognizing that age—whether youth or old age—can affect culpability and the appropriateness of a harsher sentence. Justice is not only about punishment; it is about fairness, about understanding the individual who stands before the court, and about recognizing that time itself plays a role in both accountability and rehabilitation.

For the young, crime is often a product of impulsivity, a lack of maturity, and a failure to fully grasp the consequences of their actions. Science has long shown that the human brain is not fully developed until well into the twenties, particularly the parts responsible for decision-making and impulse control. A teenager caught up in the wrong crowd, a young adult making reckless choices in desperation—these individuals may not have committed their offenses with the same level of understanding as an older, more experienced person. That does not excuse their actions, but it does change the way their culpability should be viewed.

A harsh sentence Imposed on a young person can do more than punish—it can destroy potential. The years that could be spent learning, growing, and changing are instead spent inside a system that often hardens rather than rehabilitates. A judge considering a downward departure for youth is not ignoring the crime, but rather acknowledging that a young person has a greater capacity for change. The question is not just, "What have they done?" but also, "Who could they become if given the chance?"

On the other end of the spectrum, age can also serve as a mitigating factor for older individuals. A person in their sixties or seventies facing a long sentence is not the same as a younger defendant. Prison is not just punishment for them—it is often a death sentence in slow motion. Health conditions, frailty, and the inability to defend oneself in a harsh prison environment make incarceration for the elderly far more severe than for someone in their prime.

For an older defendant, the court must consider whether prolonged incarceration serves any true purpose. Is this person a danger to society, or is their age itself a deterrent from future crime? Have they lived a lawful life for decades, only to make one critical mistake? Would an alternative punishment, one that holds them accountable without breaking them, serve justice better? These are the questions that can lead to a downward departure under 5H1.1.

Age alone is not enough to warrant leniency. A young defendant must demonstrate maturity, remorse, and a willingness to change. An older defendant must show that their health, frailty, or circumstances make a severe sentence excessive. The argument must be clear: the punishment should fit not just the crime, but also the individual.

The courts have discretion, and discretion allows for compassion where it is warranted. A downward departure based on age is not about evading justice—it is about ensuring that justice is applied fairly, with the understanding that youth and old age bring different challenges, different levels of responsibility, and different capacities for change. A one-size-fits-all sentence is not justice. The law recognizes that time, experience, and human growth all play a role in determining what punishment is truly appropriate.

CHAPTER 8

Role In The Offense (4A1.3)

In the eyes of the law, guilt is often painted with broad strokes. A crime is committed, and everyone involved is swept into the same current, regardless of how deep their hands were in wrongdoing. But justice is not meant to be blind to the details. Not everyone plays the same role in an offense, and not everyone deserves the same level of punishment. That is why the law allows for a downward departure based on a defendant's role in the crime. Under 4A1.3, proving that one's involvement was minimal or peripheral can mean the difference between a devastating sentence and a fair one.

The legal system does not always distinguish between masterminds and foot soldiers, between decision-makers and those caught in the tide of bad circumstances. The unfortunate truth is that many people facing sentencing were never the architects of the crime. Some were pressured, some were manipulated, and some played only a minor role, yet they find themselves facing the same charges as those who orchestrated the entire operation.

A minimal role means exactly that—the individual had little influence over the crime's outcome. Maybe they were a driver who never knew the full extent of the plan. Maybe they passed along a message without realizing the significance of what they were involved in. Maybe they were present but never truly participated in the criminal act itself. The law acknowledges that not all involvement is equal.

To successfully argue for a downward departure based on role, the evidence must be clear. The defendant's actions, decisions, and level of knowledge about the crime all come under scrutiny. Did they have control over what happened, or were they simply following orders? Did they profit significantly, or were they merely a bystander caught in the web? The distinction is crucial. A person whose involvement was minimal should not bear the same weight of punishment as someone who orchestrated, led, or financially benefited from the crime.

Judges consider several factors:

Level of knowledge – Did the defendant fully understand the crime, or were they kept in the dark?

Level of decision-making – Were they making choices, or simply doing what they were told?

Level of benefit – Did they gain significantly from the crime, or was their role minor?

Level of participation – Did they carry out major aspects of the offense, or were they on the sidelines?

This is where legal advocacy is crucial. A skilled defense must paint the full picture of a defendant's role, proving that their involvement does not warrant the same sentence as those who orchestrated the crime. The prosecution may argue that all players in a crime are equally culpable, but the truth is often more nuanced.

For those who truly played a minor role, a harsh sentence is not justice—it is punishment out of proportion with responsibility. The law allows for the opportunity to prove that one's hands are not as dirty as others may claim. A downward departure for role in the offense is not about making excuses; it is about ensuring that the sentence fits the crime—not just in general, but for the individual standing before the court.

CHAPTER 9

Acceptance of Responsibility (3E1.1)

In the cold, structured world of the legal system, where evidence and statutes dictate the course of justice, there exists a powerful yet often overlooked force—remorse. The ability to acknowledge one's mistakes, to own up to the choices that led to this moment, can be the difference between a crushing sentence and a path toward redemption. Under 3E1.1, the court recognizes that genuine acceptance of responsibility can warrant a downward departure, reducing the severity of a sentence for those who show true remorse.

The justice system is built on the idea that punishment should be proportionate to both the crime and the individual. But beyond the black-and-white facts of a case, there is an undeniable truth: not all defendants are the same. Some deny responsibility, refuse to acknowledge the harm they have caused, and attempt to manipulate the system to escape accountability. Others face their past head-on, accepting their actions and demonstrating a sincere commitment to change.

Judges and prosecutors take note of this distinction. They see the difference between someone who is merely going through the motions to secure a lighter sentence and someone who truly regrets their actions. Real remorse is not just words spoken in a courtroom—it is reflected in a person's demeanor, their willingness to cooperate, and their efforts to make amends.

Acceptance of responsibility is not about admitting guilt to satisfy the court—it is about proving that the defendant understands the weight of their actions. This can be shown through:

Statements of genuine remorse – A heartfelt acknowledgment of wrongdoing, not excuses or justifications.

Cooperation with authorities – Demonstrating a willingness to assist in the resolution of the case, whether by providing information or making the legal process smoother.

Efforts to make amends – Taking proactive steps to repair the harm caused, whether through restitution, community service, or personal rehabilitation.

Behavior in custody – A change in attitude, a willingness to engage in rehabilitation programs, and conduct that reflects a sincere commitment to personal growth.

However, acceptance of responsibility is not just about saying the right things—it must be backed by action. A defendant who claims remorse but continues to justify their behavior will not receive the same consideration as one who takes full ownership of their choices. The court looks for sincerity, for a real demonstration of character growth and accountability.

Judges understand that people make mistakes. Some crimes are born from desperation, poor judgment, or external pressures. But the ability to stand before the court and acknowledge those mistakes with honesty and humility speaks volumes. It shows the potential for rehabilitation, for becoming a productive member of society rather than someone who will return to crime.

A downward departure for acceptance of responsibility Is not a loophole—it is a recognition that justice should not only punish but also allow room for change. When a person genuinely regrets their actions, when they seek to right their wrongs, the law allows for leniency. Because, at its core, the legal system is not just about retribution—it is also about redemption.

CHAPTER 10

Sentencing Disparities (3553(a))

Justice is meant to be fair, yet for many defendants, fairness feels like a distant dream. Two individuals can commit the same crime, have similar backgrounds, and yet walk away with drastically different sentences. One may receive probation, while the other is handed years in federal prison. How does this happen? How can the legal system justify such inconsistency? Under 18 U.S.C. § 3553(a), courts are required to consider sentencing disparities to ensure that individuals are not punished more harshly than others in similar circumstances.

For those facing sentencing, the fear of an excessive punishment lingers like a heavy fog. They hear stories of others—people with the same charges, the same criminal history—who received lighter sentences. Some walked free with time served, while others saw their lives dismantled by excessive prison terms. The inconsistency is undeniable. Different judges, different districts, different prosecutors—these variables should not determine a person's fate, but too often, they do.

This is where § 3553(a) becomes a lifeline. The law recognizes that sentencing should not be arbitrary. It demands that courts consider whether a sentence aligns with others who have committed the same offense under similar conditions. If a defendant can demonstrate that others in comparable situations received lighter sentences, a downward departure may be warranted.

Building the Case for a Lesser Sentence

To successfully argue for a reduced sentence under § 3553(a), several key elements must be presented:

1. Comparing Similar Cases – The defense must identify cases where similarly situated defendants received more lenient sentences. These cases must involve comparable charges, criminal history, and circumstances.
2. Highlighting Sentencing Trends – If data shows that most defendants convicted of a particular crime receive a lesser sentence, this discrepancy must be brought to the court's attention.
3. Pointing Out Geographic Inconsistencies – Sentencing varies drastically between jurisdictions. A defendant should not receive a harsher sentence simply because of where their case was prosecuted.
4. Emphasizing Judicial Discretion – Judges have the power to depart from sentencing guidelines when a punishment does not align with fair sentencing practices. The argument must focus on why a lesser sentence is not just appropriate but necessary for justice.

The Reality of Sentencing Disparities

The unfortunate truth is that disparities exist. Some defendants are given leniency because they had better legal representation. Others are prosecuted in districts known for extreme sentencing. Factors unrelated to the crime—race, socioeconomic background, even the attitude of a particular judge—can influence the outcome. This is not how justice should work. The law must recognize that fairness is not just a principle; it is a requirement.

For a defendant seeking a downward departure, this is not about avoiding responsibility—it is about ensuring proportionality. The law should not be a game of chance, where fate is determined by arbitrary factors. By invoking § 3553(a), a defendant is not asking for special treatment; they are asking for the fairness that the law itself demands. A sentence should fit the crime, but it should also fit the broader landscape of justice. If others have received lighter sentences for the same actions, then the court has an obligation to acknowledge that disparity and correct it.

Justice must not be determined by luck. It must be deliberate, consistent, and fair. The law allows for that fairness, but only if defendants and their advocates fight for it.

Part 3

Legal and Circumstantial Factors to Seek a Downward Departure

In the quiet moments before sentencing, the weight of the courtroom can feel unbearable. The harsh reality sets in—the acknowledgment that your life, your future, rests in the hands of a judge who must decide whether to extend mercy or enforce punishment. It's a nerve-wracking, gut-wrenching experience. For some, the looming question is not just how long will they be sentenced, but why they should be sentenced the way the law demands. While the law is meant to be impartial, it is not blind to the deeper, more complex circumstances that shape each individual case.

The law itself offers a glimmer of hope in its recognition of legal and circumstantial factors. These factors are not mere technicalities; they are the real-life truths that speak to a person's character, their history, their intentions, and their capacity for change. These factors are the story of who you are beyond the crime you've committed. They are the reasons why, perhaps, you are not defined by your worst moment, but by the full measure of your life—its challenges, its growth, and its potential for redemption.

Legal factors such as substantial assistance to authorities, criminal history, or acceptance of responsibility are powerful arguments for a downward departure. They speak to the choices a defendant has made after the crime—whether they've assisted in the investigation, taken responsibility for their actions, or demonstrated a willingness to change. These are the decisions that show the court you are not the same person who committed the crime. You've learned, you've grown, and you are willing to face the consequences with the sincerity of someone who is striving for something better.

But beyond the legal factors, there are also circumstantial factors—elements of your personal story that are often invisible in the sterile confines of the courtroom. These include your family responsibilities, your mental health struggles, or your age—circumstances that can significantly impact your ability to cope with the harsh realities of a prison sentence. For instance, a parent with young children may be more deeply affected by a lengthy sentence than someone without family obligations. A person suffering from a mental illness may be disproportionately harmed by a prison system not equipped to provide the care they need. These are not excuses, but they are the realities that the court must consider when determining what is truly just.

The circumstances surrounding the offense can also play a pivotal role. A person who commits a crime out of desperation, under duress, or in a moment of extreme emotional distress may deserve a more compassionate sentence than someone who acted out of cold calculation or malice. Life is rarely black-and-white; crimes are often the result of a tangled web of pressures, misjudgments, and personal pain. When the court acknowledges these nuances, it allows for justice that is more than just a formulaic application of the law—it allows for a fairer, more empathetic response to the complex factors that shape human behavior.

For those seeking a downward departure, the emotional weight of this argument is undeniable. You are not just asking for leniency; you are asking for understanding. You are offering the court the full scope of who you are—not just as a defendant, but as a person. You are asking the court to consider not only the crime but the broader context in which it occurred and the person who stands before them today.

This chapter is a reminder that while the law must maintain order and justice, it is also a living, breathing reflection of human experiences. And within that space, there is room for compassion, for mercy, and for recognizing that a sentence should not only punish—it should also offer a chance for rehabilitation and growth. The law, in its deepest sense, is about more than retribution; it is about shaping lives, offering second chances, and ensuring that justice is truly just.

CHAPTER 11

Minor Role in the Offense (3B1.2)

The courtroom is full of scrutiny, and every decision feels like a weight that could tip your future in an irreversible direction. You sit in the defendant's chair, heart pounding in your chest, and the weight of your mistakes presses down on you. The charge is real, the consequences are heavy, and you know what the law says about those who commit crimes. But there's more to the story than what meets the eye. You were involved, yes, but your role—your actual participation in the offense—was not as large, not as significant, as the prosecution would like to suggest. In fact, the truth is that you were a minor participant, and you now stand before the judge, hoping that this fact will not be overlooked.

There is an undeniable power in being able to demonstrate that your role in the offense was less significant than that of others involved. Under U.S. Sentencing Guidelines Section 3B1.2, a downward departure can be granted when a defendant can show that their role in the crime was minimal or peripheral. This is not an excuse for the offense, but it is a critical piece of the puzzle that could help shift the balance toward a fairer and more just sentence.

Understanding The Power Of Your Role

The law doesn't treat all participants in a crime equally. It recognizes that some individuals may play a much larger role in planning or executing the offense, while others are dragged in, coerced, or manipulated into a situation that is not entirely their doing. Demonstrating that you were a minor participant doesn't erase your involvement, but it can show the court that you did not deserve the same harsh punishment as those who were the masterminds or more active perpetrators.

A minor role does not mean a lack of responsibility, but it does mean that you weren't driving the car. You didn't pull the trigger or plan every detail. Instead, you might have been swept along by events, acting out of fear, desperation, or ignorance. Maybe you didn't have the power to make key decisions, or maybe you were involved only because of someone else's pressure or manipulation. Whatever the reason, the truth is that you were not at the center of the crime—you were, at most, a piece in a larger puzzle.

Demonstrating a Minor Role

Successfully demonstrating your minor role in the offense can be challenging, as it requires proving a lack of influence over the crime. This isn't an easy claim to make, and the burden of proof falls on you. In order to make a compelling case, the following factors can be essential:

1. Coercion or Manipulation – If you were coerced, pressured, or misled into participating in the crime, this is an important factor. If you can show that you were manipulated or influenced by another participant, you can argue that you played a far less significant role. The more you can prove that you had no independent control over the crime, the better the chance you have to show your limited involvement.
2. Lack of Leadership or Control – If you were not in charge, did not organize the crime, and did not influence its planning or execution, these facts can support your case. Perhaps you followed someone else's orders or acted out of fear, or maybe you were not present for key stages of the offense.
3. Mitigating Circumstances – If there are factors that show you were not fully aware of the crime's severity or consequences at the time, they can strengthen your argument. For example, if you were a young person, under the influence of drugs or alcohol, or otherwise impaired, these circumstances can help explain your diminished role in the offense.
4. Testimony or Evidence of Your Limited Involvement – Any corroborating evidence, such as statements from co-defendants or evidence that shows you did not take an active role in executing the crime, can significantly bolster your case.

The Emotional Impact Of A Minor Role

Facing the fact that you've been involved in something criminal is devastating enough. But to stand before the court and argue that your role wasn't as significant as others' can feel like a double-edged sword. You are still asking for forgiveness, even if you didn't fully deserve the consequences that came with the crime. For some, admitting that they were a minor participant is a painful truth—one that confronts their own pride, their own identity. It's hard to accept that the events that led you here were beyond your control, but it's important to recognize that the law understands human complexity. It understands that sometimes, people find themselves involved in things that are far bigger than they ever realized.

Showing that you were a minor participant doesn't erase the damage done, but it does present the opportunity for the court to view your actions with more compassion. It's not about trying to escape responsibility; it's about ensuring that your sentence is fair, based on the level of your involvement. And when the court acknowledges your minor role, it creates space for justice that isn't blind, but one that considers your individual actions, your intentions, and your potential for change.

The Path Forward

In the end, demonstrating a minor role in the offense is not about escaping punishment. It's about ensuring that punishment is proportional and just. If you were involved, but not to the degree that others were, it is important for the court to recognize that. A downward departure based on your minor role could lead to a sentence that reflects the reality of your actions, not just the crime as a whole. It could be the difference between years of unnecessary hardship and a sentence that allows for rehabilitation, growth, and a second chance at life.

As you stand there before the judge, remember that your story isn't just about the crime you committed. It's about understanding your role, taking responsibility, and seeking fairness in a system that sometimes forgets the humanity of those involved. Your minor role is a part of that story—and with the right legal argument, it can be the key to unlocking a more just and compassionate outcome.

CHAPTER 12

Lack of Criminal History (4A1.3)

The weight of your past is a heavy burden to carry, especially when the decision of your future rests in the hands of those who can only judge you by what they see in front of them. But in the midst of all this, there is something that can play a pivotal role in your case—something that offers a glimmer of hope in the form of a clean or minimal criminal history. The lack of a criminal record can be one of the most powerful arguments you have when seeking a downward departure in your sentencing.

The law often considers a person's history when determining the severity of a sentence. A record littered with prior offenses might lead to harsher penalties, reflecting the belief that repeat offenders pose a higher risk to society. But what if your past is unblemished? What if you've never been in trouble with the law before this moment? This clean slate—or even a minimal criminal history—can demonstrate to the court that your crime is not a reflection of a longstanding pattern of behavior. It becomes a part of your story that tells the court, This is not who I am. It offers the possibility for the judge to see you in a different light, as someone who has made a mistake but has not previously lived a life of criminality.

The Power Of A Clean Record

Your lack of criminal history doesn't erase the offense, but it can offer the court a reason to show leniency. When the law is considering a sentence, it often evaluates the defendant's background, including whether they have committed prior offenses. A lack of criminal history or a minimal history can indicate that the offense was an anomaly—a rare lapse in judgment—rather than a part of a pattern of criminal behavior. This can create a compelling case for a reduced sentence, as the court may view you as someone who is more likely to rehabilitate and integrate back into society without repeating your mistake.

In U.S. Sentencing Guidelines Section 4A1.3, the lack of a significant criminal history is recognized as a valid reason for a downward departure. The rationale is that individuals with little to no criminal history are less likely to pose a continuing threat to society, making them eligible for a more lenient sentence. If you can demonstrate that you have no past convictions—or a minimal criminal record, such as only minor infractions—it gives weight to the argument that this offense was a deviation from your character, not the culmination of a criminal life.

Demonstrating The Importance Of A Clean Record

Successfully leveraging your lack of criminal history in your sentencing requires more than just presenting the fact that you've stayed out of trouble. It's about framing your history as evidence of your potential for reform. Here's how you can make that argument effectively:

1. A Pattern of Law-Abiding Behavior – You need to show that, throughout your life, you have generally followed the law. This could include work history, community involvement, or any other evidence that demonstrates you are an upstanding individual. Your clean record isn't just a list of no offenses; it's a testament to your character and the choices you've made before this incident.
2. One-Time Mistake – Emphasize that the crime you committed was a one-off, a mistake in judgment, rather than the culmination of a life of crime. If you can demonstrate that this incident is out of character for you and not reflective of your usual behavior, it makes the argument for a downward departure much stronger.
3. Commitment to Rehabilitation – A clean record also signals that you are someone who is capable of change. If you have already begun to take steps toward rehabilitation—such as enrolling in programs, seeking counseling, or making efforts to better yourself—this shows that you are not the same person who made the mistake. It strengthens the argument that you can learn from this incident and reintegrate into society as a law-abiding citizen.

4. Character References – Support your argument with testimonies from family, friends, employers, or others who can vouch for your character. These references can attest to your lack of criminal history and the positive traits that have defined you up until this point. They provide an outside perspective on the person you are and can humanize your case in ways that statistics cannot.

The Emotional Strain Of A Clean Record In A Moment Of Weakness

Having a clean criminal record can also be a source of great pride, and yet, facing a sentence that could diminish that record is devastating. It feels like the culmination of your life's work—the careful decisions, the moments when you could have taken a wrong turn but didn't—being erased by one mistake. There's an emotional toll that comes with the weight of that realization. But it's important to remember that this mistake does not define you. You are not the sum of a single moment in time, and the law, at its best, recognizes that.

A clean or minimal criminal record speaks to a life that has largely been lived without brushes with the law, and this should not be disregarded. When you stand before the judge, the lack of a criminal history isn't just a piece of paper—it's the story of the person you were before this mistake. It's the story of a person who has the potential to move beyond this error, to learn from it, and to re-enter society as someone who has been forever changed, but not defined, by it.

The Path Forward: Embracing Redemption

The fact that you have no prior convictions doesn't mean that your crime should be excused. But it does suggest that you are someone who can be rehabilitated, someone whose offense is a singular event that doesn't necessarily reflect your life as a whole. The court, in considering your lack of criminal history, may decide that you deserve a chance at redemption—a chance to learn from this moment, to grow, and to eventually reintegrate into society without the heavy hand of punishment that a harsher sentence might bring.

If the judge sees that this offense is out of character for you, that you have been law-abiding before and after this incident, they may grant a downward departure, reflecting the belief that your path forward holds more promise than punishment. It's about ensuring that the sentence fits not just the crime, but the person who committed it—the person you were before, the person you are now, and the person you can become with the right support and understanding.

In the end, a clean or minimal criminal record doesn't guarantee mercy, but it offers a foundation on which the court can build an argument for leniency. It says, This was a mistake, but I am more than the sum of this mistake. It's a chance for the judge to see your potential for change and to consider that you might just need guidance, not punishment, to get back on the right track.

CHAPTER 13

Coercion Or Duress (5K2.12)

How Coercion or Duress Can Be Used as a Factor for a Downward Departure

When we talk about crime, it's easy to assume that all offenders acted with a clear intent, that they made deliberate decisions and chose the path they walked. But in some cases, the reality is far more complicated. What if you were not acting of your own free will? What if external forces pushed you into committing a crime, forcing you into a position where you had no choice? This is where the concept of coercion or duress comes into play.

Coercion or duress is a powerful factor that can be considered by the court in determining whether a downward departure from a sentence is appropriate. In legal terms, coercion or duress means that you were forced to commit a crime due to the threat of harm or actual harm being inflicted upon you or someone you care about. Under the U.S. Sentencing Guidelines Section 5K2.12, if you can demonstrate that you committed a crime because you were under duress or coercion, this can influence the judge's decision to reduce your sentence.

The Weight Of Coercion Or Duress: When Choice Is Taken Away

In a world where personal responsibility and free will are heavily emphasized, the idea of duress can seem foreign. But what happens when your own safety or the safety of someone you love is on the line? The law recognizes that, in certain circumstances, individuals may be pushed into situations where committing a crime becomes a means of survival. When faced with the threat of immediate harm—whether physical, emotional, or psychological—the ability to make rational, clear-headed decisions becomes clouded by fear.

Imagine standing in a moment where a loved one is threatened with violence unless you carry out a crime. What would you do? The legal system understands that in these moments, your ability to make choices freely is severely compromised. If you can demonstrate that you were under duress or coercion, it means you were not acting with the criminal intent typically associated with criminal conduct. Instead, you were responding to threats that manipulated you into committing the offense.

What Is Coercion Or Duress In Legal Terms?

In legal terms, coercion or duress refers to a situation in which a person is forced to engage in criminal conduct because they are threatened with imminent and severe harm if they refuse. There are specific elements that need to be proven for this defense to apply:

1. Imminence of the Threat – The threat of harm must be immediate and unavoidable, leaving no reasonable alternative but to commit the crime.
2. Severity of the Harm – The harm threatened must be serious and real. It can be physical harm, but it can also involve threats to your family, your livelihood, or your mental and emotional well-being.
3. Lack of Opportunity to Escape – There must be no way to safely avoid the harm without committing the crime. In other words, you had no other viable options to protect yourself or those you care about.
4. Proportionality of the Crime – The crime you committed must be directly related to the threat you were facing. In other words, the act of committing the crime must have been a direct response to the duress or coercion you experienced.

If you can demonstrate these factors, you may be able to argue that your criminal behavior was not voluntary but rather a survival mechanism forced upon you by the threat of harm. This, in turn, may convince the court to impose a more lenient sentence, as your actions were not driven by criminal intent but by fear and necessity.

Emotional And Psychological Impact Of Coercion Or Duress

What often gets overlooked in cases of coercion or duress is the emotional and psychological toll it takes on the individual. Imagine the mental weight of being forced to make a decision that goes against everything you believe in because you fear for your own life or the lives of those you love. It's not just the act itself, but the psychological trauma of knowing you have no other choice. The emotional distress of being under constant threat can be just as damaging as the physical harm you might face.

This is not about excusing the crime, but about understanding the immense pressure that coercion or duress places on an individual. The moment of the crime may be one of intense anxiety, fear, and confusion, where you acted in a state of crisis. The fear of immediate harm can overwhelm every sense of morality, turning you into someone who is simply trying to survive in an unbearable situation.

Understanding this, the court may be more inclined to offer a downward departure in sentencing, recognizing the severe mental and emotional strain you were under. It's about acknowledging that, in that moment, you were not fully in control of your actions and that your response was a reaction to an overwhelming and unjust situation.

Proving Coercion or Duress in Court

While the idea of coercion or duress may seem like a compelling defense, it's important to understand that it's not always easy to prove in court. It's a delicate balance of presenting clear evidence that supports your claims. Here are some ways to strengthen your case:

1. Witness Testimony – If there were witnesses who can attest to the threats made against you, their testimony could be crucial. People who were present during the coercion or duress can help corroborate your story.
2. Physical Evidence of Harm – Evidence of any physical harm you may have suffered as a result of the threat can lend weight to your claim. This could include medical records, photographs, or other documentation of abuse or threats.

3. Credible Documentation of Threats – If you have any form of written or recorded evidence, such as threatening phone calls, text messages, or emails, it can serve as vital evidence of the coercion or duress you were under.
4. Psychological or Expert Testimony – Expert testimony from psychologists or mental health professionals can help explain the psychological toll that duress can have on a person's ability to make rational decisions.

The Hope For A Lighter Sentence

When facing a potential sentence for a crime you committed under duress or coercion, it may feel like there is little hope. You may feel guilty, torn, and ashamed, but it's crucial to understand that your situation is not one of malice or criminal intent. The court recognizes the unique circumstances that force individuals into committing crimes under pressure. If you can show that your actions were the result of external coercion, the court may find it appropriate to impose a lesser sentence, one that takes into account the extraordinary circumstances surrounding your behavior.

In the end, coercion or duress is not an excuse, but it is a valid factor that can be used to argue for a downward departure. The law understands that sometimes, a person's actions are dictated not by their will but by the threats of harm they face. If you can demonstrate that you acted under duress or coercion, you offer the court the opportunity to show mercy and understand the complexity of your situation. Your sentence should reflect not only the crime committed but the overwhelming force of circumstances that led you there—allowing you a chance to move forward without the harshest consequences.

CHAPTER 14

Victim's Conduct (5K2.10)

How the Victim's Actions Might Have Contributed to the Offense

In the realm of criminal law, the focus is often on the actions of the defendant—the person accused of committing the crime. The legal system typically evaluates the defendant's intent, the evidence presented, and the seriousness of the offense. However, there is another important element to consider: the role of the victim. While this may seem counterintuitive, there are circumstances in which the conduct of the victim can be taken into account when determining the severity of the sentence.

Under U.S. Sentencing Guidelines Section 5K2.10, a judge may consider the victim's conduct as a factor that could justify a downward departure from the prescribed sentence. If the victim's behavior contributed significantly to the events leading up to the crime, this may provide a compelling argument for why the defendant should not face the full weight of the law. This concept recognizes that actions of the victim can sometimes provoke, escalate, or otherwise contribute to the commission of the offense. It offers a nuanced approach to sentencing, one that acknowledges the complexity of human interactions and the many factors that influence criminal behavior.

Understanding The Impact Of The Victim's Conduct

When we think about a crime, we often assume that the victim is entirely innocent—an unwitting target of the defendant's actions. However, life is rarely so simple. People's behavior and actions can inadvertently provoke a chain of events that leads to harm. For instance, what if the victim escalated the situation by provoking the defendant with threats or violence? What if the victim's actions led to a direct confrontation that resulted in the crime? While this doesn't absolve the defendant of responsibility, it does paint a more complete picture of the circumstances surrounding the crime.

The concept of the victim's conduct acknowledges that not all offenses happen in a vacuum. Sometimes, a defendant's response to the victim's actions—whether in self-defense, retaliation, or a moment of heightened emotion—can significantly alter the severity of the crime. A downward departure is not automatic in these cases, but if the victim's actions played a substantial role in provoking or escalating the situation, the court may consider this when determining the appropriate sentence.

Victim's Conduct and Its Influence on the Crime

The victim's conduct can take many forms, and it's important to understand how these actions may contribute to the offense in a meaningful way. Below are some key factors that may influence the judge's decision to consider the victim's conduct in sentencing:

1. Provocation And Escalation Of Violence

If the victim actively provoked the defendant—whether through verbal insults, physical confrontation, or threats—this could be a factor that influences the severity of the crime. For example, in a situation where both parties were involved in a heated altercation, and the victim escalated the violence, it may be argued that the defendant's actions were a direct response to the victim's conduct. The idea is not to excuse the defendant's behavior, but to recognize that the defendant may have acted out of heightened emotions or in self-defense, rather than from premeditated intent to cause harm.

2. Victim's Role In The Crime

In some cases, the victim may have contributed to the circumstances that led to the offense. For instance, if the victim played an active role in facilitating or encouraging criminal conduct, the defendant's participation may have been an unfortunate byproduct of that involvement. A judge may take this into account when determining the appropriate sentence. This could apply in cases where a victim was involved in illegal activity with the defendant, thereby setting the stage for the commission of the crime.

3. Mutual Conflict Or Previous Encounters

In some situations, the defendant and the victim may have had a history of conflict, which can impact the way the offense is viewed. If the defendant's actions were a continuation of prior altercations or a response to a long-standing dispute, the judge may consider the cumulative impact of those interactions. The nature of the relationship between the defendant and the victim—whether it's one of mutual hostility or provocation—could influence the severity of the crime.

4. Victim's Consent Or Participation

In certain crimes, the victim's consent or participation may reduce the perceived culpability of the defendant. For example, in cases involving certain offenses, such as fraud or theft, if the victim willingly participated in the transaction or failed to take necessary precautions, the defendant's actions might not be viewed as entirely malicious. While consent doesn't absolve a crime, it may reduce the severity of the offense and, by extension, the sentence. This could be particularly relevant in cases where the victim was complicit in some way, either knowingly or unknowingly, in the commission of the crime.

The Psychological Impact Of Victim Behavior

While legal factors are important in evaluating the role of the victim in a crime, it's also necessary to consider the psychological impact that the victim's conduct may have had on the defendant. Emotions like fear, anger, humiliation, or betrayal can influence a defendant's response to the victim. In some cases, the victim's behavior might push the defendant to act in ways they would not have otherwise. A defendant who feels personally attacked or threatened may react impulsively, without considering the consequences.

When examining the victim's conduct, the court may also take into account the mental and emotional state of the defendant at the time of the crime. For example, if the defendant was under extreme duress or stress because of the victim's actions, this might have impacted their ability to think rationally or make informed decisions. The court may consider how the victim's conduct led to a loss of self-control on the part of the defendant and factor this into the sentencing.

Proving The Victim's Conduct In Court

As with other sentencing factors, it is crucial to provide evidence to support the claim that the victim's actions contributed to the offense. Some key forms of evidence include:

1. Witness Testimony – Statements from witnesses who observed the victim's behavior or interactions with the defendant can provide valuable insight into how the victim's actions may have contributed to the crime.

2. Documented Evidence of Prior Conflicts – If there is a history of conflict between the defendant and the victim, this documentation could be used to demonstrate that the victim's conduct was not isolated, but part of an ongoing pattern.

3. Physical Evidence – In cases where the victim provoked violence or escalated the situation, physical evidence, such as injuries to either party, can help corroborate claims that the victim played a role in the offense.

4. Psychological Reports – If the victim's conduct had a direct emotional or psychological effect on the defendant, expert testimony from mental health professionals may help demonstrate the impact of the victim's actions on the defendant's state of mind.

The Path to a Reduced Sentence

The purpose of considering the victim's conduct in sentencing is not to excuse the defendant's actions, but to provide a fuller understanding of the dynamics that led to the crime. By recognizing that both the victim's and defendant's actions played a role, the court can ensure that the sentence reflects the complexities of the situation. If the victim's conduct significantly contributed to the offense, it may be grounds for a downward departure from the usual sentence.

While not every case involving victim conduct will lead to a reduced sentence, understanding the context in which a crime occurred is essential in ensuring that justice is served in a fair and balanced manner. When the victim's actions have had a meaningful impact on the crime, this could open the door to a more lenient sentence—one that acknowledges the broader circumstances and provides the defendant with an opportunity to move forward from the experience.

CHAPTER 15

Effect on the Community or Family (3553(a))

How the Impact of Your Sentence on Your Family or Community Could Justify a Reduction

In the pursuit of justice, the law often focuses on punishing individuals for their wrongdoings. Yet, as many defendants know, the effects of a sentence reach far beyond the person standing in the courtroom. A conviction and subsequent sentence can ripple out, affecting not just the defendant, but their family, their community, and even society at large. It is here that the sentencing guidelines allow room for compassion, offering an opportunity for the defendant to present how the impact of their punishment could have far-reaching and disproportionate consequences on their loved ones or the community in which they live.

Under U.S. Sentencing Guidelines 3553(a), a judge may take into consideration the effect a sentence would have on the defendant's family or community when deciding whether a downward departure is appropriate. The law recognizes that the punishment of one person can sometimes lead to a cascade of consequences that are felt by many others. These consequences—whether emotional, financial, or social—are often outside the control of the defendant but nonetheless profound in their effect. Therefore, the sentencing process gives the court discretion to consider these factors and weigh them against the need for punishment.

The Weight of Family Ties and Responsibilities

When a defendant's family is depending on them for emotional support, financial stability, or caregiving, the impact of a lengthy sentence can be devastating—not only to the defendant but to those left behind. Many individuals convicted of crimes are fathers, mothers, spouses, or children. Their absence can create a void that is hard to fill, particularly if they were the primary provider or caregiver in the family.

In many cases, a defendant's family members may be reliant on them for basic needs, such as food, shelter, and healthcare. A sudden disruption in the family unit due to incarceration can cause a ripple effect that alters the lives of those who had no part in the crime. Spouses may lose income and stability, children may grow up without their parents, and elderly family members may be left without support during their time of need.

Judges can consider these factors when evaluating the sentence. In cases where the defendant is the sole provider or primary caretaker for a vulnerable family member, such as a young child or an elderly parent, the effect of a prison sentence may be deemed overly harsh in light of the collateral consequences on their family's well-being. The idea here is not to excuse the crime but to recognize the broader impact that incarceration can have on innocent people, particularly those who depend on the defendant for their livelihood or care.

The Ripple Effect On The Community

Beyond the family, a sentence can have profound consequences on the community where the defendant lives and works. The community can be affected in many ways—whether through the loss of a valued member of the workforce, the disruption of local services, or the emotional toll it takes on people who know and care for the defendant.

For example, a defendant who has been an active member of their community—perhaps by volunteering, mentoring at-risk youth, or working in a local business—may have contributed in ways that are not easily quantifiable. A lengthy sentence could pull them away from these community activities, causing a gap that is hard to fill. In such cases, the community may suffer as a whole, and the impact of losing that individual could outweigh the benefits of their punishment.

Judges may also consider the social consequences of a sentence on the local area. For instance, if the defendant is a business owner, their incarceration may lead to the closure of a business that employs people and contributes to the local economy. The community may lose more than just a person; they may lose a sense of stability, a local economy anchor, or a key player in the neighborhood's social fabric.

The Emotional Toll on Family and Community

The emotional toll of a sentence is not always tangible, but it can be deeply felt by those closest to the defendant. Families are often left to carry the burden of separation, dealing with the loss of a loved one not only physically but emotionally. Parents may be heartbroken to see their child sent to prison; children may struggle with feelings of abandonment, anger, and confusion. Spouses may face a future alone, dealing with the hardship of keeping their family together while also dealing with the stigma and challenges of having a loved one incarcerated.

In the community, there are often more subtle emotional effects. Friends, colleagues, and mentors who have witnessed the defendant's positive contributions to society may feel a profound sense of loss and disappointment. People who have invested in the defendant's growth and rehabilitation may feel as though they have been left behind as well. The loss of an individual who has impacted others' lives in meaningful ways creates a ripple effect that can alter the dynamics of the community as a whole.

Arguments for a Reduced Sentence

In light of the emotional, financial, and social consequences that a prison sentence can impose on families and communities, a judge may decide that a downward departure is justified. This decision is not about excusing the crime but about considering the broader impact that incarceration would have on innocent individuals.

1. Financial Hardship on the Family

If the defendant is the primary earner in the household and their incarceration would leave the family without financial support, a downward departure might be warranted. In cases where children or elderly family members rely on the defendant for survival, the court may determine that a lesser sentence would allow the defendant to continue supporting their family in meaningful ways.

2. Caregiving Responsibilities

If the defendant is responsible for caring for a dependent family member—such as an elderly parent or a disabled child—the court may find that their absence would cause undue hardship on the family. The defendant may be able to fulfill these responsibilities in ways that are more beneficial to the family outside of a correctional facility.

3. Community Impact

If the defendant plays a crucial role in their community, such as being an educator, mentor, or local leader, the loss of their presence may be felt deeply. If the defendant's positive contributions to the community are substantial, a reduced sentence could allow them to continue those efforts and make a greater impact.

4. Rehabilitative Contributions

Sometimes, the defendant's efforts to turn their life around may be a significant factor. If the defendant has shown a deep commitment to rehabilitation—through education, therapy, or volunteer work—this can demonstrate their potential to continue contributing positively to their family and community. A downward departure may allow them the chance to keep pursuing these rehabilitative goals outside of prison.

The effect of a sentence on a defendant's family and community is not something that can be easily quantified, but it is a factor that has the power to influence the judge's decision. In considering these collateral consequences, the court can balance the need for punishment with the recognition that sometimes, the impact on innocent people—particularly vulnerable family members or communities—is enough to justify a reduction in the sentence. When faced with the broader ripple effects of incarceration, the court may find that a downward departure serves both the interests of justice and the needs of society. It's not about leniency but about ensuring that the punishment fits the crime, while also considering the weight of the consequences on those who had no part in the offense.

CHAPTER 16

Health Conditions (3553(a))

Using Serious Health Issues to Argue That a Lighter Sentence or Alternative Form of Sentencing Is Appropriate

When a defendant faces serious health conditions, the implications of a lengthy sentence can go beyond the immediate consequences of incarceration. Chronic illness, physical or mental health problems, and medical conditions can drastically affect a person's quality of life. In such cases, judges may consider the individual's health as a factor in determining the severity of their sentence. This is particularly true when the defendant's health issues could significantly worsen in a correctional setting or when they are unable to receive appropriate care while incarcerated. The health of a defendant is an essential component in sentencing decisions, as it speaks to the question of whether the punishment fits the individual and their circumstances, not just the crime itself.

Health Conditions And The Impact On Sentencing

Health conditions that are serious and chronic in nature may justify a downward departure, or even an alternative form of sentencing, depending on the situation. For instance, if a defendant is suffering from a terminal illness or has a condition that requires specialized treatment that cannot be adequately provided in prison, it may be unreasonable to impose a traditional sentence. Health concerns become a pivotal argument for those who advocate for lighter sentences or different forms of punishment that are more suitable for the defendant's condition.

In these cases, U.S. Sentencing Guidelines 3553(a) allows judges to consider the defendant's health when determining an appropriate sentence. The key focus here is the severity of the illness and the extent to which it would negatively impact the defendant's ability to serve a traditional sentence in a prison setting. For instance, a defendant with a life-threatening illness such as cancer may require regular medical treatment, which may not be available in a prison. In such cases, imprisonment could lead to a rapid deterioration of health, leaving the defendant in worse condition than they were before incarceration.

Terminal And Chronic Illness

One of the most compelling arguments for a downward departure based on health concerns is the presence of terminal illness. When a defendant is diagnosed with a terminal condition—whether it be cancer, AIDS, or a degenerative disease like ALS (Amyotrophic Lateral Sclerosis)—the question arises as to whether their remaining time would be better spent outside of prison. The emotional toll of knowing that one has limited time to live can be devastating, and the effects of incarceration can worsen the already fragile health of the individual.

When considering whether to grant a departure, judges must balance the defendant's crime with the life they have left to live. For some, the harshness of a prison sentence may not be justified when weighed against the severity of their health condition. A downward departure in these cases could involve reducing the sentence or even granting a sentence that allows the defendant to serve time at home with medical care, such as house arrest or other forms of compassionate release.

In situations where the defendant's illness is progressive, and their prognosis is poor, the court may also consider a reduced sentence to allow the individual to receive more appropriate care or simply have the chance to be with loved ones in their final months. This approach acknowledges that the individual's suffering from their condition may be punishment enough, and that further deprivation could be inhumane.

Medical Needs In Prison

Another factor in determining the appropriateness of a downward departure is the capacity of the prison system to meet the defendant's medical needs. While prisons have medical facilities, they are often ill-equipped to deal with serious health conditions that require specialized care or constant monitoring. For example, a defendant who is diabetic, epileptic, or requires dialysis may not receive the level of care necessary to manage their condition effectively while incarcerated.

This lack of access to adequate healthcare in prisons can lead to serious complications, including unnecessary pain, suffering, or even death in extreme cases. A defendant with such a condition may argue that a prison sentence would only exacerbate their health problems, and that an alternative form of punishment would allow them to manage their condition more effectively. In cases where the prison cannot adequately provide for the defendant's medical needs, the court may determine that a downward departure is warranted. This departure could involve placing the defendant in a medical facility or home confinement where they can receive proper care.

Mental Health Conditions And Sentencing

Health conditions are not always physical; mental health issues also play a significant role in sentencing decisions. Mental health conditions such as severe depression, schizophrenia, or bipolar disorder can affect a defendant's ability to function in a prison environment. In some cases, a defendant's mental health condition might even be the underlying cause of the criminal behavior. For instance, a person suffering from untreated mental illness may not fully understand the consequences of their actions or may have been unable to control their behavior due to their condition.

In these situations, sentencing can take into account how a mental health condition may impede the defendant's ability to serve a prison sentence effectively. Prisons are not typically equipped with the resources necessary to provide proper mental health treatment, which can lead to worsening conditions for the defendant. If a defendant suffers from a mental health condition that is severe and requires continuous treatment or medication, the court may decide that a lighter sentence or a different form of sentencing—such as placement in a mental health facility—would be more appropriate than a traditional prison sentence.

Compassionate Release And Alternative Sentencing

Health conditions can also be a strong argument for compassionate release, which is a form of early release from prison for defendants who are suffering from serious illnesses or health conditions. Under the First Step Act and other federal regulations, defendants who are terminally ill or have chronic medical conditions that cannot be treated effectively in prison may qualify for compassionate release. This process allows the court to consider the defendant's condition and reduce the sentence to a more humane alternative, such as home confinement or supervised release.

For example, if a defendant has a debilitating condition that prevents them from performing daily activities and requires constant care, compassionate release may allow them to spend their final days with family members or receive medical treatment in a more appropriate setting. Compassionate release recognizes the inherent humanity in every individual and acknowledges that the purpose of punishment is not to cause unnecessary suffering.

Argument For A Lighter Sentence

A defendant can argue that the impact of their health condition on their ability to serve a prison sentence justifies a downward departure. When presenting this argument, the defendant should provide documentation from medical professionals outlining the severity of their condition, the treatment required, and the implications of incarceration. Furthermore, it is important to demonstrate how a traditional prison sentence may not be the best way to manage their condition and that an alternative form of punishment would allow for more effective care while still serving the goals of justice.

The Role Of Compassion In Sentencing

Ultimately, the consideration of a defendant's health in sentencing is not about minimizing their crime or excusing their behavior. Rather, it is about ensuring that the punishment is appropriate for the individual circumstances, including their health condition. By considering the impact of health on a defendant's ability to serve a sentence, the court can make decisions that are more humane and just. This is especially important for those suffering from conditions that affect their ability to live a normal life, and for those who may not be able to receive the necessary care in a correctional facility.

In cases where health issues are severe, courts may find that an alternative form of sentencing—such as home confinement, a medical facility, or compassionate release—could better serve the purposes of punishment and rehabilitation while still accounting for the need for justice. Health conditions, when weighed appropriately, have the potential to lead to more compassionate and appropriate sentencing, helping to ensure that the punishment truly fits the individual's circumstances and not just the crime itself.

CHAPTER 17

Involvement In The Offense By Others (5K2.10)

If Others Were More Involved In The Offense, This May Support A Downward Departure

When a defendant's role in the commission of a crime is peripheral or minor, the court may consider the involvement of others who played a more substantial role in determining the severity of the sentence. In many cases, the full scope of the offense and the participants involved can shed light on the defendant's actual level of culpability. If others were more involved in orchestrating or carrying out the offense, the judge may decide that a downward departure from the sentencing guidelines is appropriate for the defendant.

The argument here is that, while the defendant may have committed a crime, their actions were less central to the overall offense, and others may have had a far more significant impact. This could potentially lead to a reduced sentence for the defendant, as it highlights the imbalance between their involvement and the roles played by others in the commission of the crime.

Understanding The Role Of Co-Conspirators

In any criminal case, there is a fundamental distinction between those who are actively involved in committing the crime and those who may have played a lesser or more passive role. In instances where the offense involved multiple individuals, the involvement of co-conspirators can weigh heavily in the court's decision to grant a downward departure.

The defendant who had a more limited or peripheral role in the crime may argue that the true perpetrators were others who were more directly responsible for the criminal conduct. This could include situations where the defendant was merely a follower or played a supporting role while others were the masterminds or took on the primary responsibilities. If the defendant's involvement is significantly less than that of other participants, they may argue that their sentence should reflect their level of culpability, which was comparatively minimal.

This argument requires careful examination of the facts surrounding the offense. It may involve a detailed breakdown of how the crime was committed, with attention to who planned and executed the criminal conduct. If the defendant's role was limited to a minor or tangential aspect of the crime, they can present evidence to support their claim for a downward departure, emphasizing their relative lack of responsibility for the overall offense.

Evaluating The Defendant's Role In The Crime

One of the most important aspects of this argument is an accurate portrayal of the defendant's role in the offense. The court will look closely at the actions of the defendant compared to the actions of others involved. For example, if the crime involved a group of people working together, the court will consider who took the lead in planning or executing the offense. A defendant who was less involved in decision-making or who did not actively participate in key aspects of the crime may have a stronger case for a downward departure.

The defendant may present evidence that they were Influenced by or coerced by others who played a larger role in the crime. This could involve situations where the defendant was intimidated or pressured into participating or where they were less aware of the full scope of the criminal enterprise. This aspect can significantly affect the court's perception of the defendant's culpability and willingness to grant a downward departure.

Examples Of Limited Or Peripheral Involvement

There are many examples where a defendant's involvement in a crime is peripheral, and the involvement of others is far more substantial. For instance, in a drug trafficking operation, one defendant may have been merely a transporter or courier, responsible only for moving drugs from one location to another, while others were responsible for the distribution and organization of the entire operation. In such a case, the defendant could argue that their role was limited and that others were primarily responsible for the logistics and distribution of the drugs.

Similarly, in cases of fraud, one individual might have been responsible for organizing the scheme, while another defendant played a minor role in executing a small part of the plan. The defendant with the minor role can argue that their involvement was secondary to the actions of the main perpetrator, and thus their sentence should reflect this disparity.

In a theft or burglary case, a defendant who was only tangentially involved—such as a lookout or a driver—may also seek a downward departure. If others were responsible for the planning and execution of the crime, the defendant can demonstrate that their involvement was limited, and that the primary blame rests on those who played a more active role in carrying out the offense.

Coercion Or Influence By Others

In some cases, the defendant may have been heavily influenced or coerced by others to participate in the offense. This is particularly true in situations involving peer pressure, gang involvement, or instances where the defendant was threatened with harm if they did not comply with the plans of others. If the defendant can demonstrate that their involvement was the result of coercion or duress, this can support their argument for a reduced sentence. They can show that they were not a willing participant but were instead pushed into committing the crime by more dominant individuals.

This defense may require supporting evidence, such as testimony from the defendant or others involved, or documentation showing the defendant's vulnerability to influence. The judge will consider how much control the defendant had over their actions and whether they were simply following the lead of others who were more dominant or authoritative.

Influence Of Co-Conspirators In Group Crimes

When crimes are committed by groups, the court may also evaluate the relationship between the defendant and the other participants. In organized criminal activity, the leader of the group may be the one who orchestrated the crime, while others may have participated out of loyalty, fear, or coercion. In these situations, the defendant's role is critical in determining their sentence. If the defendant played a relatively passive role, following the instructions of a leader or co-conspirator, this can be presented as a mitigating factor in seeking a downward departure.

For example, if a defendant was recruited into a criminal enterprise by someone they trusted or feared, they may argue that their role was not voluntary or that they did not have the agency to make independent decisions about their participation. The defendant can argue that they were led to believe their actions were necessary or that they were simply part of a group effort in which they played a minimal part.

Presenting The Argument For A Downward Departure

In seeking a downward departure, the defendant must present evidence and arguments that show their role was not central to the offense. This might involve a detailed review of the case facts, including the roles of others, witness statements, and any available evidence that sheds light on the defendant's limited involvement.

Defense attorneys can emphasize the disparity between the defendant's actions and those of other participants, demonstrating that the defendant should not be held equally accountable for the full scope of the crime. They can also point to any mitigating circumstances, such as coercion or influence by others, that support the defendant's claim for a reduced sentence.

The Role Of The Court In Assessing Involvement

The court must carefully evaluate the degree of involvement of all participants in the offense. The defendant's role should be measured against the severity of the crime and the extent to which others were involved. In some cases, a downward departure may be warranted if the defendant's actions were minimal compared to those of others involved in the crime. By considering the participation of others, the court can ensure that the defendant's sentence is proportional to their actual involvement in the offense.

In cases where others played a more significant role in the crime, the defendant may seek a downward departure to reflect their more peripheral involvement. This argument relies on showing that the defendant's actions were limited, secondary, or influenced by the actions of others. By highlighting the disparity between their role and the roles of others, and by demonstrating coercion or a lack of agency, the defendant can make a compelling case for a reduced sentence. A downward departure in these situations helps ensure that the punishment fits the crime, taking into account the varying levels of responsibility among those involved.

CHAPTER 18

Unwitting Participation In The Offense (5K2.16)

Demonstrating That Your Participation Was Unwitting Or Without Full Knowledge Of The Criminal Nature Of The Act

In some cases, a defendant may be able to demonstrate that their involvement in a crime was not intentional or fully understood at the time of the offense. The concept of unwitting participation in a crime is rooted in the argument that the defendant did not possess the necessary criminal intent or knowledge to fully understand the illegal nature of their actions. In situations like these, a defendant can make the case for a downward departure by showing that they were unaware of the criminal activity they were involved in and that their participation was, in fact, unintentional or unknowing.

For many defendants, the idea of being unwittingly involved in a crime can be deeply emotional. It can be an experience marked by feelings of betrayal, confusion, or vulnerability. The realization that one's actions, which may have been done with no malice or intent to harm, have led to criminal charges can be overwhelming. In these moments, the defense strategy focuses on explaining that the defendant lacked the requisite criminal knowledge or understanding, and that their participation was not driven by any desire to commit a criminal act.

Understanding Unwitting Participation

The legal definition of unwitting participation is rooted in the concept of mens rea, which refers to the mental state or intent required to commit a crime. Most criminal offenses require not just the physical act (actus reus) but also a guilty mind (mens rea). In cases of unwitting participation, the defendant argues that they did not have the requisite mental state to commit the crime. This argument can be particularly powerful when the defendant's role in the offense was passive or peripheral, and they were unaware of the full scope or nature of the criminal conduct.

Unwitting participation is often seen in cases where the defendant is misled, deceived, or manipulated by others. For example, a defendant may have been led to believe that they were participating in a legitimate business venture or social activity, only to later discover that the actions they took were, in fact, criminal in nature. In such cases, the defendant may argue that they were unknowingly assisting in illegal activity, whether through ignorance or misunderstanding, and that their actions were not driven by criminal intent.

Examples Of Unwitting Participation

One common example of unwitting participation is seen in cases of individuals unknowingly carrying or transporting illegal goods, such as drugs or stolen property. In these cases, a defendant may have been told that they were simply helping someone out, not realizing that the items they were transporting were part of a larger criminal operation. The defendant may have believed that they were innocently running an errand or completing a task, without any knowledge of the illicit nature of the goods involved.

Similarly, in fraud cases, a defendant may have unknowingly participated in an illegal scheme by being misled by co-conspirators or by being given inaccurate information. For instance, a person may have been employed by a business that was, unbeknownst to them, involved in fraudulent activities such as falsifying records or misleading clients. The defendant's participation in these activities may have been limited to performing their job duties, without ever fully understanding that their work was supporting criminal behavior.

The Role Of Deception In Unwitting Participation

Deception is often a key factor in cases involving unwitting participation. A defendant may have been deliberately misled by others who were more deeply involved in the criminal activity. Co-conspirators may have used manipulation, lies, or concealment to keep the defendant unaware of the true nature of their actions. This can occur in a variety of criminal contexts, including drug trafficking, money laundering, or even large-scale fraud schemes.

In these situations, the defendant may not have had any reason to question the legitimacy of the actions they were involved in. They may have been told that the activities were lawful or simply not been given enough information to realize that they were participating in a crime. For example, in a drug trafficking case, a defendant may have been asked to transport what they were told were harmless goods, only to later discover that they were unknowingly carrying illegal drugs.

Challenges Of Proving Unwitting Participation

While unwitting participation can be a compelling argument for a downward departure, it can also be difficult to prove. The defendant must provide sufficient evidence to show that their involvement was truly unintentional and that they did not have knowledge of the criminal nature of the act. This often requires the defendant to provide testimony explaining their lack of awareness and to present any available evidence—such as witness testimony, communications, or other documentation—that supports their claim of ignorance.

Additionally, the court may consider the defendant's background and whether they should have known about the illegal nature of their actions. In cases where the defendant had previous experience with criminal behavior, it may be harder to convince the court that their participation was truly unwitting. However, in cases where the defendant had no prior knowledge of the offense or was not involved in any criminal conduct before, their argument may carry more weight.

The Emotional Impact Of Unwitting Participation

For many defendants, the emotional weight of unwitting participation is significant. The realization that their actions, which may have been motivated by good intentions or mere compliance with others, have led to serious legal consequences can be overwhelming. This emotional turmoil is often compounded by feelings of betrayal—by the individuals who manipulated them, by the justice system, or even by themselves for not recognizing the warning signs sooner.

In many cases, the defendant may feel an overwhelming sense of guilt or confusion, struggling to understand how they became involved in a criminal act they never intended to commit. This emotional burden is further compounded by the fear of the unknown—fearing how a conviction may affect their future, their reputation, and the lives of their loved ones. The desire for a downward departure in such cases is not just about reducing the sentence; it is about seeking justice and a recognition of the defendant's lack of criminal intent.

The Court's Consideration of Unwitting Participation

When determining whether a downward departure is warranted based on unwitting participation, the court will carefully examine the facts of the case. The judge will consider the defendant's knowledge of the crime, the level of their involvement, and whether others were more responsible for the criminal conduct. The judge may also take into account any efforts by the defendant to mitigate the harm caused by their actions, such as voluntarily reporting the crime, cooperating with authorities, or making restitution to victims.

Ultimately, the court will determine whether the defendant's participation in the offense was truly unwitting or if they should have known that their actions were illegal. This evaluation is crucial in deciding whether a downward departure is justified, as the court must balance the defendant's lack of criminal intent with the need for accountability.

Conclusion

In cases where a defendant can demonstrate unwitting participation in a crime, they may be able to make a strong argument for a downward departure from the sentencing guidelines. This argument is built on the premise that the defendant did not fully understand the criminal nature of their actions and was not acting with criminal intent. While proving unwitting participation can be challenging, it is a valid defense that may lead to a more lenient sentence, particularly when the defendant's involvement was minimal, and they were manipulated or deceived by others. By emphasizing the lack of knowledge and intent, the defendant can seek a fairer outcome, one that reflects their true level of responsibility in the offense.

Part 4

CHAPTER 19

The Safety Valve – A Gateway to Relief from Harsh Mandatory Minimums

Part 1: What Is the Safety Valve and Why It Matters

For thousands of federal defendants, the courtroom is not a place where justice feels balanced—it is a place where mandatory minimums overshadow individuality, growth, and second chances. A person may have made a mistake. They may have committed a federal crime. But too often, their sentence isn't determined by who they are—it's determined by a rigid formula that offers no consideration for personal transformation, family obligations, or the complexity of their involvement.

That's where the safety valve comes in.

Created by Congress as part of the Violent Crime Control and Law Enforcement Act of 1994, and expanded in 2018 under the First Step Act, the safety valve provision was designed to provide relief to first-time, low-level, nonviolent offenders facing harsh mandatory minimum sentences in federal court. It is the law's way of saying: not everyone deserves to be buried beneath a decade of federal time.

The safety valve exists under 18 U.S.C. § 3553(f) and its companion, U.S. Sentencing Guidelines § 5C1.2. If a defendant meets all five statutory requirements, the judge is permitted to sentence them below the statutory mandatory minimum—even if they pled guilty or were convicted at trial. The importance of this cannot be overstated. It can be the difference between 10 years and 18 months. The difference between a young parent going home or losing a decade with their children. The difference between rebuilding or being buried by the system.

What makes the safety valve unique is that it doesn't require a cooperation agreement. A defendant doesn't have to "snitch." They don't have to testify. They don't even have to help get anyone else indicted. They only have to tell the truth about their own involvement.

But qualifying isn't automatic. The law requires that five very specific conditions be met. These are not general suggestions—they are strict statutory criteria. If a defendant fails even one, the safety valve doesn't apply.

Here are the five requirements as listed in § 3553(f):

1. The defendant has no more than 4 criminal history points (excluding 1-point offenses), and no 3-point violent or drug trafficking convictions.
2. The defendant did not use violence or credible threats of violence, nor possess a firearm or dangerous weapon in connection with the offense.
3. The offense did not result in death or serious bodily injury to any person.
4. The defendant was not an organizer, leader, manager, or supervisor in the offense.
5. Before sentencing, the defendant truthfully provided to the government all information and evidence they have concerning the offense and related conduct.

Each of these criteria has its own complexities. Federal prosecutors may contest eligibility, and the burden is often on the defense to prove the requirements are satisfied. The courts have interpreted these provisions through years of case law, and navigating the nuances takes careful planning, smart strategy, and the right presentation of evidence.

This chapter will walk you through each requirement, one at a time, using real-world application, critical federal case law, and practical insight. You'll learn how to prove eligibility, how the courts interpret key terms like "use of violence" or "truthfully provided information," and how to position yourself—or a loved one—for the best possible outcome under this provision.

The safety valve can be a second chance. It can be the door back home. For many defendants, it's not just a legal option—it's the lifeline.

In the next part, we'll begin with Requirement One: Criminal History Limitations—what counts, what doesn't, and how a few points can change everything.

Part 2: Criminal History and the Safety Valve (18 U.S.C. § 3553(f)(1))

Understanding the Point System That Can Make or Break Your Chance at Relief

Of the five safety valve requirements, the very first one is often where eligibility is gained—or lost.

Under 18 U.S.C. § 3553(f)(1), a defendant is only eligible for the safety valve if they do not have:

More than four criminal history points, excluding 1-point offenses,

Any 3-point offense that is a violent offense, or

Any 2-point violent offense that is prior to the current case.

This criterion is built on the criminal history point system found in U.S.S.G. Chapter 4, Part A, and if misunderstood, it can derail a valid safety valve claim before it even starts. To apply this provision effectively, we must break down what counts, what doesn't, and how to avoid disqualification by points.

How Criminal History Points Are Calculated

The Sentencing Guidelines assign points to a defendant's prior convictions. These points are totaled to place the defendant into a Criminal History Category (I–VI), which affects the recommended sentencing range. For safety valve purposes, the concern is not your category—but your exact number of points, and the type of convictions behind them.

The points are generally assessed as follows:

3 points for each prior sentence of more than 13 months of imprisonment (U.S.S.G. §4A1.1(a))

2 points for each prior sentence of at least 60 days but not more than 13 months (U.S.S.G. §4A1.1(b))

1 point for each prior sentence less than 60 days, such as fines or probation, up to a limit of 4 total 1-point offenses (U.S.S.G. §4A1.1©)

But not all points count the same when applying the safety valve.

What § 3553(f)(1) Actually Says (Post–First Step Act)

After the First Step Act of 2018, Congress revised this section to be stricter. The current law reads that the defendant must not have:

More than 4 criminal history points, excluding 1-point offenses,

Any prior 3-point offense that is violent or a drug trafficking offense,

Any prior 2-point violent offense.

This means that:

1-point convictions don't count toward the 4-point cap.

You can have four 1-point offenses and still qualify.

But one 3-point violent conviction automatically disqualifies you.

And even one 2-point violent conviction can also bar eligibility.

The language "excluding 1-point offenses" has created confusion—but courts have clarified its meaning.

Case Law Insight: United States v. Lopez, 998 F.3d 431 (9th Cir. 2021)

In United States v. Lopez, the Ninth Circuit confirmed that when applying § 3553(f)(1), 1-point offenses are not counted toward the 4-point total. This means a defendant with four separate 1-point misdemeanors can still qualify for the safety valve, assuming all other criteria are met.

However, if a defendant has even one prior 3-point conviction that involved violence or drug trafficking, they're disqualified. It doesn't matter how old it is or whether it seems unrelated—it matters how it's scored under the Guidelines.

Important Distinction: Violent vs. Non-Violent Convictions

The terms "violent offense" and "drug trafficking offense" are key here. Courts often use 18 U.S.C. § 16 or the Sentencing Guidelines' definitions to interpret what counts as a "crime of violence."

A violent offense generally involves:

The use, attempted use, or threatened use of physical force against another person

Or a felony that, by its nature, involves a substantial risk of force being used

Drug trafficking offenses include:

Convictions for distribution, manufacture, or possession with intent to distribute

Even if no violence occurred in the case

A prior simple possession case might not count—but possession with intent to distribute almost certainly does.

Practical Application: Avoiding Disqualification

To preserve safety valve eligibility:

Scrutinize every conviction in your criminal history.

Work with your attorney to determine how it's scored under U.S.S.G. §4A1.1.

Challenge improperly scored convictions.

Understand whether the prior offense qualifies as "violent" under federal standards.

Your defense team may need to submit a sentencing memorandum with case law and records arguing that a prior conviction is not violent or not drug-related.

Part 3: No Use or Possession of Violence, Threats, or Firearms (18 U.S.C. § 3553(f)(2))

Why the Absence of Violence Is Crucial for Safety Valve Relief

The second requirement under the safety valve statute is simple in wording but strict in practice. It states that the defendant must have:

"did not use violence or credible threats of violence or possess a firearm or other dangerous weapon (or induce another participant to do so) in connection with the offense."

18 U.S.C. § 3553(f)(2)

This provision makes it clear: if violence, threats, or weapons were involved in your offense—or even reasonably associated with your role—you may be disqualified from receiving a reduced sentence under the safety valve. But the phrase "in connection with the offense" carries legal depth and has been the subject of decades of litigation. Let's break it down.

The Legal Meaning of "Use," "Threat," or "Possession"

This requirement bars eligibility if the defendant:

Used violence

Made a credible threat of violence

Possessed a firearm or dangerous weapon

Caused or encouraged someone else to do any of the above

Each of these disqualifying conditions has been shaped by how courts interpret the words "use," "possess," and "in connection with."

1. **"Use of Violence" or "Threats of Violence"**

The violence doesn't need to result in injury. A threat that is "credible"—meaning it reasonably caused fear—is enough to disqualify. Even if no weapon was shown, words or gestures interpreted as threatening by the court can count. This includes threats made to co-conspirators, witnesses, or victims.

2. **"Possession" of a Firearm**

Possession doesn't mean the gun has to be on your body. Courts have upheld safety valve disqualification when:

The firearm was in the same house, car, or stash location as the drugs.

The gun was owned by someone else but you had access to it.

The gun was part of the operation's tools, even if unused.

The key term here is "in connection with the offense"—if the firearm could be seen as protecting the drugs, money, or operation, that's enough for denial.

United States v. Nelson, 222 F.3d 545 (9th Cir. 2000)

In Nelson, the Ninth Circuit clarified that constructive possession of a firearm is sufficient to block safety valve relief. The defendant didn't carry the gun, but it was in a closet near drug supplies. That proximity and its apparent purpose—protection of the drugs—was enough to deny the safety valve, even without active use.

This ruling echoes the common prosecutorial argument: if a gun was within reach and connected to drug activity, it disqualifies you.

United States v. Wilson, 105 F.3d 219 (5th Cir. 1997)

In Wilson, the court stated that for the firearm to disqualify someone, it must have "some purpose or effect with respect to the offense." This reinforces that mere ownership of a gun isn't always enough. If the gun is legally owned and not connected to the criminal act, your defense may argue it doesn't trigger § 3553(f)(2).

But this is a tough defense to win. The court will look at:

Proximity of the gun to the drugs

Whether it was loaded

Whether it was accessible

Whether it served a protective function

Key Considerations for the Defense

1. Was the firearm legally owned and stored separately from the crime?
2. Can you prove the firearm had no relation to the offense?
3. Can you show the weapon was someone else's and not under your control?
4. Was the weapon ornamental, inoperable, or clearly not used in furtherance of the crime?

If you didn't know a gun was present, or it belonged to a co-defendant without your consent or control, your attorney should fight hard to argue non-possession under case law and fact-specific evidence.

The Possibility of Co-Conspirator Weapons or Violence

Even if you never touched a gun or made a threat, the government may argue you "induced" another participant to do so, or that you participated in a conspiracy where a weapon was present. In this case, the court may find that you indirectly facilitated the presence of a weapon or benefited from it.

That's why your exact role in the offense is key.

If a co-defendant was armed and you had no knowledge, the court may allow safety valve relief—but if the court believes you knew or should have known, disqualification is likely.

Tactical Advice for Defense

Challenge weapon possession aggressively—File motions disputing that a firearm was "connected" to the offense.

Present strong evidence of separation—If the weapon was legally owned, locked away, or in another room, emphasize that.

Clarify your role—Prove you didn't induce, support, or benefit from violence or weapons in any way.

A sworn statement, witness testimony, or even expert testimony on gun use in drug cases may help persuade the judge that § 3553(f)(2) should not block your access to the safety valve.

Part 4: No Death Or Serious Bodily Injury Resulting From The Offense (18 U.S.C. § 3553(F)(3))

Why Harm to Others Can Block the Path to Safety Valve Relief

The third requirement under the safety valve provision is straightforward in its language, but like the others, its legal application must be interpreted through case law and federal sentencing precedent.

Under 18 U.S.C. § 3553(f)(3), the defendant is ineligible for safety valve relief if:

- "the offense resulted in death or serious bodily injury to any person."

This criterion exists to separate nonviolent and low-impact federal crimes from those that result in actual physical harm. The law makes clear that if the offense caused serious injury or loss of life, even unintentionally, the court cannot consider reducing the sentence below the statutory minimum—regardless of the other circumstances. The safety valve is meant for nonviolent offenders. If someone was physically hurt or killed in connection with the offense, the safety valve closes.

Defining "Serious Bodily Injury"

The term "serious bodily injury" is not interpreted loosely. According to U.S.S.G. §1B1.1, Application Note 1(L), it is defined as:

> "injury involving extreme physical pain or the protracted impairment of a function of a bodily member, organ, or mental faculty; or requiring medical intervention such as surgery, hospitalization, or physical rehabilitation."

This includes:

Broken bones

Gunshot wounds

Knife injuries

Major car crashes during flight from law enforcement.

Injuries from overdoses linked directly to the defendant's conduct (especially in drug distribution cases).

It does not include minor scrapes, bruises, or emotional distress. The injury must be significant and usually documented with hospital or law enforcement records.

Key Case Law: United States v. Martinez, 339 F.3d 759 (8th Cir. 2003)

In Martinez, the Eighth Circuit denied safety valve relief to a defendant involved in a drug deal that ended in gunfire and injury, even though the defendant never fired a weapon. The court ruled that since the offense conduct—including the planning and setting of the deal—created conditions that resulted in serious bodily injury, the defendant was disqualified under § 3553(f)(3).

This case established that proximate causation matters. Even if the defendant didn't personally injure someone, if the offense created a chain of events that led to serious injury, the court can deny safety valve relief.

Injury Caused by Co-Defendants

A critical point: the court may attribute the injury to the defendant even if someone else caused it—if it occurred during and in furtherance of the jointly undertaken criminal activity. This falls under the broader scope of relevant conduct in sentencing.

So, if a co-defendant pulls a weapon and hurts someone during a robbery, drug deal, or home entry—and you were present or played a role in setting the event in motion—courts may hold you accountable and deny safety valve eligibility.

Does Intent Matter?

Intent does not control this provision. Even if the injury was accidental, or the defendant had no intention to hurt anyone, the result—death or serious bodily injury—disqualifies them.

This can lead to tragic consequences for well-meaning defendants. For example, in drug cases involving fentanyl or other powerful substances, if someone overdoses and dies or is hospitalized, courts often view the offense as having "resulted" in death or injury—even if the defendant had no idea how strong the drug was or didn't personally deliver it.

Medical Evidence and Defense Strategy

To counter this, the defense must:

Scrutinize the medical reports – Was the injury truly "serious"? Did it meet the criteria under §1B1.1?

Challenge causation – Did the defendant's conduct actually cause the injury, or was it an independent event?

Use expert testimony – In overdose or injury cases, medical experts can sometimes clarify whether the injury meets the legal threshold for "serious bodily injury."

Separate the defendant's conduct – Show that the defendant played no role in the conduct that led to injury, particularly when the harm came from co-defendants acting outside the scope of the joint plan.

Examples of Disqualifying and Non-Disqualifying Scenarios

Disqualifying:

A customer overdoses on drugs provided by the defendant and is hospitalized.

A co-defendant assaults someone during a robbery the defendant helped plan.

The defendant flees a drug bust and crashes into another vehicle, causing injury.

Potentially Non-Disqualifying:

Emotional trauma without physical injury.

Minor scrapes or bruises that didn't require medical attention.

Co-defendant acts on their own, without direction or participation from the defendant.

This provision places great weight on the outcome of the offense. The courts are less concerned with your intentions and more focused on whether your actions—or your codefendants'—ended with someone physically harmed. Judges are given no discretion if this condition is triggered. If serious bodily injury occurred, you cannot qualify for the safety valve, no matter how compelling the other circumstances are.

Part 5: Not An Organizer, Leader, Manager, Or Supervisor (18 U.S.C. § 3553(F)(4))

How Your Role in the Crime Determines Access to the Safety Valve

The fourth requirement of the safety valve statute places a spotlight on your role in the offense. It asks the court to determine whether you were just a participant—or whether you were one of the people running the show. According to 18 U.S.C. § 3553(f)(4), the safety valve is only available to defendants who:

> "was not an organizer, leader, manager, or supervisor of others in the offense, as determined under the sentencing guidelines and was not engaged in a continuing criminal enterprise."

The key issue here is aggravated role. The safety valve excludes those who exercised control over others or played a decision-making, leadership, or supervisory role in the criminal activity. This requirement ensures that relief is reserved for low-level, nonviolent offenders, not the architects or bosses behind organized crime or drug operations.

The determination is guided by U.S.S.G. §3B1.1, which details how courts assign role enhancements during sentencing.

The Sentencing Guideline: U.S.S.G. §3B1.1 – Aggravating Role Enhancements

Under §3B1.1, a defendant's offense level may be increased based on their role:

+4 levels if the defendant was an organizer or leader of a criminal activity involving five or more participants or that was otherwise extensive

+3 levels if the defendant was a manager or supervisor of such an operation

+2 levels if the defendant managed or supervised even one other participant

If the judge determines at sentencing that you deserve a role enhancement under §3B1.1, you are automatically disqualified from safety valve eligibility under § 3553(f)(4). This applies even if all the other requirements are satisfied.

But there's a difference between being involved and being in charge. Many defendants participate in criminal offenses—delivering packages, running errands, making introductions—without having the authority or control that makes them a leader or organizer. Courts are careful to look at the substance of the defendant's role, not just their title or visibility.

Key Factors the Courts Consider (from U.S.S.G. §3B1.1, Application Notes):

1. Decision-making authority

2. Recruitment of accomplices
3. Claim to a larger share of the profits
4. Participation in planning or organizing the offense
5. Degree of control and authority over others
6. Nature and scope of the criminal activity

If you had no authority over anyone else, made no major decisions, didn't recruit anyone, and simply played a passive or mechanical role, you may qualify. The judge must find, by a preponderance of the evidence, that you did not organize, lead, manage, or supervise anyone.

Case Law Insight: United States v. Delgado, 653 F.3d 729 (9th Cir. 2011)

In Delgado, the Ninth Circuit emphasized that a "manager" is someone who exercises control over at least one other participant, not just someone who manages an object or transaction. The court reversed a role enhancement where the defendant handled logistics but had no authority over anyone else.

This case illustrates the importance of who you managed—not what you managed. If you didn't give orders, didn't direct others, and didn't structure the crime, you may still qualify for the safety valve.

United States V. Martinez, 584 F.3d 1022 (11th Cir. 2009)

In Martinez, the court upheld a leadership enhancement where the defendant recruited couriers, organized pickups and drop-offs, and coordinated travel for a drug trafficking ring. Because of that control over others, he was deemed an organizer—and thus, ineligible for safety valve relief.

This case shows that recruitment and delegation are red flags for disqualification. Even if the crime itself was nonviolent, leadership is disqualifying.

Role in the Offense vs. Role in the Conspiracy

Another nuance in safety valve cases is the difference between your role in the overall conspiracy versus your role in the specific offense of conviction. Some courts focus only on the latter. That means even if the conspiracy was large, your personal involvement may still be considered minor.

In United States v. Munoz, 430 F.3d 1357 (11th Cir. 2005), the court held that the defendant's leadership in a broader conspiracy did not disqualify him from safety valve relief If his leadership was not proven in connection with the specific offense he was being sentenced for.

Common Mistakes That Lead to Disqualification

Taking responsibility for others during arrest or sentencing

Allowing yourself to be portrayed as the "one in charge" without correction

Not challenging a PSR (Pre-Sentence Report) that labels you as a supervisor

Not understanding how minor actions—like coordinating a ride—could be seen as supervisory

Defense Strategy for Preserving Safety Valve Eligibility

1. Challenge any role enhancement during sentencing if the facts do not support it
2. Avoid language or admissions that suggest you led or managed others
3. Provide evidence (letters, testimony, conduct during the crime) that shows you acted alone or were following instructions
4. Object to any unsupported conclusions in the PSR that suggest you had a leadership role
5. Request specific findings from the judge to clarify your role, especially when the government attempts to stretch facts into a leadership theory

If your role was limited, passive, or mechanical, and you didn't direct others, the court may find that you do not meet the disqualifying criteria under § 3553(f)(4), preserving your eligibility for the safety valve.

Part 6: Truthfully Providing All Information And Evidence To The Government (18 U.S.C. § 3553(F)(5))

Telling the Whole Truth Without Having to "Cooperate"

The fifth and final requirement of the safety valve is often the most misunderstood—and the most important. It reads:

- "not later than the time of the sentencing hearing, the defendant has truthfully provided to the Government all information and evidence the defendant has concerning the offense or offenses that were part of the same course of conduct or of a common scheme or plan..."
  - **18 U.S.C. § 3553(f)(5)**

This requirement is often referred to as the "debriefing" requirement or the "tell all" clause. But here's what's critical: it is not cooperation in the traditional sense. You are not required to testify, make controlled buys, or help prosecute anyone else. You are only required to truthfully and completely tell the government everything you know about your own involvement and related conduct.

If you do this—no matter whether the government uses the information—you fulfill the requirement. If you withhold anything or lie, you risk losing eligibility, even if you meet the other four factors.

The Purpose Behind The Provision

Congress designed § 3553(f)(5) to reward honesty. The theory is simple: if you're a low-level, nonviolent offender and you're willing to own up to what you did, the judge should be allowed to sentence you below the mandatory minimum. It's not about punishing silence, but about rewarding full disclosure.

This is your chance to explain the full picture—to be honest about your conduct, your role, and anything connected to your crime. Even if the government doesn't believe your information is useful, they cannot deny you safety valve relief if you were truthful.

What Does "Truthfully Provided" Mean?

"Truthfully provided" does not mean "perfect memory" or "cooperative witness." It means:

You told the whole truth about your actions and role.

You didn't lie, minimize, or hide parts of the conduct.

You provided everything you personally know about related activity.

This includes:

Your own actions

Other participants you dealt with directly

Locations of meetings or transactions

Methods of operation you were aware of

Any knowledge about broader schemes you were a part of

If you honestly don't know the answer to something, you can say that. What matters is that you're not holding anything back that you do know.

Case Law Insight: United States v. Thompson, 76 F.3d 166 (7th Cir. 1996)

In Thompson, the court emphasized that a defendant cannot pick and choose what to share. Truthfulness requires full and complete disclosure. Even if the withheld detail seems small, any omission can be grounds for denial. The defendant in that case admitted to some conduct but denied knowledge of key details that were later proven true. The court found he was not credible, and denied safety valve relief.

This case sets a standard: partial honesty is not enough.

Timing Matters: Before the Sentencing Hearing

You must complete your debrief before sentencing begins. If you wait too long, you're disqualified—even if you eventually tell the truth. Courts are strict about this deadline. Judges will not delay sentencing just to give you more time to qualify.

Debriefings usually take place with your attorney present, in a controlled environment—often with a prosecutor and law enforcement officer. Your lawyer can and should be there with you.

What If the Government Disagrees?

If you and your attorney believe you've told the truth, but the government claims you didn't, the burden is on you to prove eligibility. The judge—not the prosecutor—makes the final call.

This is where credibility becomes everything. If your version of events is consistent, honest, and backed by facts—even if the government doesn't find it helpful—the court can still find that you were truthful.

United States v. Mejia-Pimental, 477 F.3d 1100 (9th Cir. 2007) confirmed this: the court held that the usefulness of the information is irrelevant—truthfulness is the only standard.

What If You Don't Know Much?

You can still qualify. Some low-level defendants simply don't have much information about the broader operation. That's okay—as long as what you do provide is complete and truthful.

You don't get disqualified for being too small to know everything. But you do get disqualified for pretending you don't know when you actually do.

Protecting Yourself During the Debrief

Never go into a debriefing alone—always have your attorney present.

Review your case thoroughly—you want to be as accurate as possible.

Stick to what you know—don't guess or make statements you can't support.

Be honest about your limits—if you truly don't know something, say so.

Don't minimize or embellish—your credibility is your most valuable tool.

A smart legal team will prepare you thoroughly for this process, protect your rights during the debrief, and help you document your truthfulness in case the court needs to decide eligibility later.

Part 5:

CHAPTER 20

Rule 35 – The Quiet Door That Opens After Sentencing

Part 1: What Is Rule 35 and Why It Matters

For most people sentenced in federal court, the final bang of the gavel feels like the end. The sentence is read, the paperwork is signed, and the door to freedom slams shut for years—sometimes decades. But what many people don't realize is that in certain rare and powerful cases, there is a door that opens after sentencing. That door is Rule 35.

Rule 35 of the Federal Rules of Criminal Procedure allows for a sentence reduction after sentencing under two specific and very different conditions:

1. Rule 35(b): Upon the government's motion, for a defendant who provides substantial assistance after sentencing.
2. Rule 35(a): To correct a clear error within 14 days of sentencing.

Both sections are narrow. They aren't automatic. They aren't controlled by the defense. And most importantly—they're often misunderstood.

Rule 35 is not about appealing your sentence. It's not about challenging the conviction. It's about recognizing that something changed after the judge handed down your time. Maybe you cooperated more. Maybe you helped with a case. Maybe the court made a clear, provable mistake. In those instances, Rule 35 becomes the legal tool to adjust your sentence after it's already been imposed.

This chapter will focus primarily on Rule 35(b)—the most commonly used and impactful part—because it's the one that has led to the biggest sentence reductions in federal criminal history. But we will also explain Rule 35(a) and its limited scope for correcting errors.

We will cover:

What Rule 35(b) is and how it works

The government's role (and full control)

What counts as "substantial assistance"

The timing of motions—one year and beyond

Examples of successful Rule 35 reductions

What Rule 35 cannot do

Rule 35(a): Clear error corrections in 14 days

Part 2: Rule 35(B)(1) – Substantial Assistance Within One Year Of Sentencing

How Help After Sentencing Can Lead to Real Time Off

Rule 35(b)(1) is one of the few federal provisions that gives a defendant the chance to reduce their sentence after judgment has already been entered—but only under specific, government-controlled circumstances. It reads:

"Upon the government's motion made within one year of sentencing, the court may reduce a sentence if the defendant, after sentencing, provided substantial assistance in investigating or prosecuting another person."

- **Fed. R. Crim. P. 35(b)(1)**

This rule is rooted in the idea of ongoing cooperation. It gives the government a legal way to reward post-sentencing assistance that helps prosecutors build or finish a case. The court cannot act on its own—only the U.S. Attorney's Office can file the motion. If they do, the court is authorized to reduce the sentence to any extent it sees fit.

The Role of the Government: The Gatekeeper

The most important—and often frustrating—truth about Rule 35(b)(1) is this:

It starts and ends with the government.

The defense cannot file a Rule 35 motion. You can't petition the court directly. You can't demand a hearing. You can't appeal the government's refusal to file. The only way a sentence can be reduced under 35(b)(1) is if the U.S. Attorney files the motion. That makes prosecutors the gatekeepers.

Whether they file a motion depends on one thing:

Did your assistance help them?

That assistance must be:

Substantial — it made a real difference in an investigation or prosecution

Post-sentencing — it happened after you were sentenced

Actionable — it led to or supported arrests, charges, convictions, or credible leads

The government typically wants cooperation that's useful—such as testimony, information on drug networks, fraudulent schemes, conspirators, financial trails, or violent organizations.

What Counts as "Substantial Assistance"?

The definition of "substantial" isn't fixed in writing—but through court rulings and prosecutorial practices, it's come to mean useful, credible, and impactful help. That help might include:

Providing new, reliable information that leads to an indictment or arrest

Testifying in grand jury proceedings or at trial

Assisting in controlled calls, monitored meetings, or consensual recordings

Helping the government recover assets, funds, or property

Confirming information already known but strengthening their case

Even if you don't testify in court, your help may still qualify—especially if it leads to a plea deal or cooperation from another defendant. The key is whether your contribution gave the government a clear advantage in building or finishing a case.

Case Law Insight: United States v. Manella, 86 F.3d 201 (11th Cir. 1996)

In Manella, the Eleventh Circuit confirmed that a Rule 35(b) motion is entirely at the discretion of the prosecution. The court emphasized that it cannot force the government to file, and a defendant has no right to challenge the decision unless the refusal was based on unconstitutional motives, such as race or retaliation for protected speech.

This means that unless you can prove prosecutorial misconduct, you cannot sue, appeal, or demand a Rule 35(b). You have to earn it through helpful conduct—and trust that the government will honor their word if you deliver.

Timing: Within One Year of Sentencing

Rule 35(b)(1) is strictly limited to assistance provided after sentencing and within one year of the sentence date. If you help after the one-year mark, Rule 35(b)(2) applies—but that has tighter restrictions.

Within this one-year window, prosecutors have discretion to file the motion at any time—whether it's 10 days or 10 months after sentencing. Many motions come right before the one-year deadline because the government is waiting to confirm the value of the assistance or to secure convictions in the related case.

Sentence Reduction: How Much Can Be Taken Off?

There is no cap on how much time the court can remove under Rule 35(b)(1). If the government files the motion, the judge can:

Cut your sentence in half

Reduce it to the bottom of the guidelines

Or even reduce it to time served

The judge is not required to follow a fixed percentage. However, courts often look to U.S.S.G. §5K1.1 factors (used for pre-sentence cooperation) to guide how much to reduce:

1. The significance of the assistance
2. The truthfulness and completeness of the information
3. The nature and extent of the help
4. Any injury or risk the defendant faced
5. **The timeliness of the cooperation**

Practical Tips for Positioning Yourself for Rule 35(b)(1)

Keep cooperating after sentencing—a conviction is not the end of your value

Maintain regular communication with your attorney and the assigned prosecutor

Be proactive—if you have information, offer it early so prosecutors can evaluate its worth

Follow through—don't back out or go silent after giving an initial statement

Stay credible—inconsistencies can ruin your value and disqualify you

If the government agrees your help was substantial, they'll file the motion, and the judge will set a resentencing hearing. You'll be brought back to court, and the new sentence will be imposed publicly on the record.

Part 3: Rule 35(b)(2) – Sentence Reductions for Assistance After One Year

When Late Help Still Leads to Early Release

Most people assume that once the one-year mark passes after sentencing, the door to post-sentencing relief slams shut. But Rule 35(b)(2) is the exception to that rule. While more limited than Rule 35(b)(1), this subsection still allows sentence reductions after one year—but only in very specific and exceptional circumstances.

The rule reads:

- "Upon the government's motion made more than one year after sentencing, the court may reduce a sentence if the defendant's substantial assistance involved:

A. Information not known to the defendant until one year or more after sentencing;

B. Information provided by the defendant to the government within one year of sentencing, but which did not become useful to the government until more than one year after sentencing; or

© information the usefulness of which could not reasonably have been anticipated by the defendant until more than one year after sentencing and which was promptly provided to the government after its usefulness was reasonably apparent to the defendant."

- **Fed. R. Crim. P. 35(b)(2)**

This provision allows for late sentence reductions, but only when the circumstances fall under one of the three narrow exceptions above. Each requires careful timing, clear value, and a direct link between the delay and the value of the information.

Let's break down each of the three grounds.

A. Information Not Known to the Defendant Until After One Year

This applies when a defendant gains new knowledge after the one-year mark. Maybe you get a new cellmate who brags about an unsolved crime. Maybe you learn of hidden evidence, a fugitive's location, or fraud you hadn't uncovered before. If that information is new and leads to a meaningful contribution to a case, the government can file a motion even though more than a year has passed.

The key here is proving you did not know the information earlier and reported it promptly once you did.

B. Information Provided Early, But Only Became Useful Later

This is one of the more common reasons the government files a Rule 35(b)(2) motion. You gave truthful, credible information within a year of sentencing, but for whatever reason—slow investigations, delays in prosecution, sealed indictments—the government couldn't use your help until after the year passed.

Once the cooperation bears fruit—an indictment, a plea, a trial win—they can circle back and file the motion even if it's 14, 18, or 24 months later.

The crucial element here is that you cooperated within the first year, and the delay was on the government's end, not yours.

© Help That Became Valuable Later and Was Promptly Offered

This is the most nuanced of the three. It applies when the defendant didn't realize their information was useful until something happened—maybe a high-profile arrest, an indictment unseals, or they recognize someone in the news as a past associate.

As soon as the value becomes apparent, the defendant must promptly offer the information. If the help proves substantial and the government agrees, a motion can be filed even though more than a year has passed.

This section rewards responsiveness and good faith. If you delay sharing or fail to act when you know you can help, you may forfeit eligibility.

How Much Time Can Be Removed Under 35(b)(2)?

Just like with 35(b)(1), the court has full discretion to reduce the sentence by:

A few months

A year or more

Or even to time served

There is no minimum or maximum. The court considers:

How long after sentencing the help was given

What impact it had on an ongoing investigation

Whether the defendant acted promptly

Whether the cooperation involved risk or sacrifice

How truthful, complete, and reliable the defendant was

Case Law Insight: United States v. Aderholt, 87 F.3d 740 (5th Cir. 1996)

In Aderholt, the Fifth Circuit upheld a late Rule 35(b) motion filed more than a year after sentencing, where the defendant had cooperated early, but his information only became actionable much later. The court emphasized that as long as the initial cooperation was truthful and useful, and the delay in its usefulness was not the defendant's fault, the late motion was valid.

This reinforces that early cooperation can still pay off later, as long as the value eventually materializes.

Limitations of Rule 35(b)(2)

The government must still file the motion—you cannot do it yourself.

If your information is too vague or unverified, they won't move.

You must act quickly if the information becomes useful. Delay can kill the opportunity.

It cannot be used to fix other sentencing issues or errors—that's Rule 35(a).

Part 4: Rule 35(A) – Correcting Clear Sentencing Errors Within 14 Days

Your Last Chance Before the Judgment Locks In

While Rule 35(b) is about rewarding assistance, Rule 35(a) is about fixing mistakes. Specifically, it allows a judge to correct a sentence that contains a "clear error"—but there's a tight deadline. The rule states:

"Within 14 days after sentencing, the court may correct a sentence that resulted from arithmetical, technical, or other clear error."

- **Fed. R. Crim. P. 35(a)**

This section has nothing to do with cooperation or new information. It exists to fix obvious mistakes—mathematical miscalculations, misapplied enhancements, or errors that contradict the plea deal or the court's own statements. But if the motion isn't made within 14 days, the court loses all power to change the sentence under Rule 35(a).

This is a short window—and it closes fast.

What Counts as a "Clear Error"?

Not all errors qualify. Courts have interpreted "clear error" narrowly. It must be something:

Obvious on the record

Contradictory to the law or guidelines

Not requiring new evidence or re-litigation

A mistake that everyone agrees is wrong, but wasn't caught in time

Examples include:

A judge miscalculates the guideline range

A sentence imposed is higher than what the court stated verbally

A condition of supervised release was mistakenly applied

A mandatory minimum was imposed despite eligibility for safety valve

A supervised release term exceeds the statutory maximum

This rule is not a second chance to reargue sentencing issues, present new facts, or file a reconsideration. If the court must hold a hearing or take new testimony, it doesn't qualify under Rule 35(a).

Timing Is Everything: 14 Days Means 14 Days

The rule gives 14 days from the oral pronouncement of sentence. That includes weekends and holidays. There are no extensions, no exceptions, and no restarts. If you miss the deadline, the court has no jurisdiction to act under Rule 35(a).

Courts have consistently held that even one day late is fatal to the motion.

Case Law Insight: United States v. Abreu-Cabrera, 64 F.3d 67 (2d Cir. 1995)

In Abreu-Cabrera, the Second Circuit affirmed that Rule 35(a) motions must be based solely on obvious errors, not disputed facts or reconsidered judgments. The court made clear that even if the judge regretted the sentence, unless there was a clear and demonstrable error, they couldn't change it.

This reinforces that Rule 35(a) is a tool for correction, not re-argument.

How to Use Rule 35(a) Effectively

File quickly—your attorney should review the sentence immediately after court

Focus on errors that are objective and provable

Include the transcript or sentencing memo as evidence

Do not attempt to relitigate judgment or sentencing discretion

Defense attorneys often pair Rule 35(a) motions with objections to the Presentence Report (PSR) or written motions for clarification to create a paper trail that shows the court's sentencing error.

Rule 35(a) Is Not an Appeal Substitute

If you believe your sentence was legally wrong, disproportionate, or unfair, the proper route is a direct appeal—not a Rule 35(a) motion. This rule is not meant to second-guess the judge's reasoning. It's there to fix black-and-white errors, like saying "120 months" when the judge meant "100 months," or imposing a sentence that exceeds the statutory maximum by mistake.

Part 5: Making Rule 35 Work for You – Practical Strategy and Real-World Hope

Turning Quiet Help into Freedom

By now, it's clear that Rule 35 isn't a promise—it's a possibility. It's not a tool you control directly, but it's one you can position yourself to benefit from. Whether your goal is to reduce time through post-sentencing assistance (Rule 35(b)) or correct a clear court mistake (Rule 35(a)), the key to making this rule work is knowledge, timing, and strategic preparation.

Let's bring it all together and look at how defendants across the country have successfully used Rule 35 to change the trajectory of their lives—and how you or your loved one can do the same.

Real-Life Examples of Rule 35 in Action

Case 1: A Courier Who Kept Quiet—Then Spoke Up

A 25-year-old woman convicted for transporting narcotics refused to cooperate before sentencing, fearing retaliation. After her 120-month sentence was imposed, she decided to talk. She gave truthful details about stash house locations and participants in a conspiracy that the government hadn't fully mapped out. Seven months after sentencing, the prosecutor filed a Rule 35(b)(1) motion. The judge reduced her sentence to 60 months.

Case 2: Assistance That Paid Off Late

A man convicted in a white-collar conspiracy shared information within months of sentencing, but the lead defendant in the fraud wasn't indicted until two years later. The government credited the original assistance as "critical" and filed a Rule 35(b)(2) motion. The court reduced his 87-month sentence to 36 months.

Case 3: A Judge's Error—Spotted Just in Time

A defendant was safety valve eligible, but the court overlooked it and imposed the 10-year mandatory minimum. The defense filed a Rule 35(a) motion with a transcript showing the court misunderstood the record. Within 14 days, the judge corrected the error and re-sentenced him to 70 months, which was the bottom of the guidelines.

Tips to Maximize Rule 35 Opportunities

1. **Don't Wait to Be Asked**

If you have real information—even if you didn't cooperate before sentencing—offer it. Many Rule 35(b) motions are born from post-sentence cooperation.

2. **Document Everything**

Your attorney should keep detailed records of every offer to assist, every debrief, and every outcome. When prosecutors file the motion, they rely on this documentation.

3. **Communicate with the Prosecutor Professionally**

Your legal team should always be respectful, honest, and clear. Build a reputation for credibility. One lie can end the discussion forever.

4. **Be Patient—but Be Vigilant**

Prosecutors often wait to file Rule 35(b) motions until an arrest, trial, or plea is secured from the person you helped them target. Stay in touch with your attorney during that window.

5.

6. File Early for Rule 35(a)

If your sentence contains a clear, obvious error, move quickly. That 14-day window is firm. Once it passes, Rule 35(a) is off the table.

What Rule 35 Cannot Do

It cannot fix unjust laws—only correct clear errors or reward help

It doesn't apply if the government refuses to file a motion, unless refusal was based on illegal bias

It doesn't reopen your entire sentencing—only the sentence itself, and only for specific reasons

It doesn't apply to every kind of sentence (e.g., restitution, supervised release length usually can't be modified under Rule 35)

The Bigger Picture

Rule 35 is part of a broader system that, though often rigid, leaves cracks for mercy. In federal court, most avenues for relief close fast. But Rule 35 remains one of the few post-sentencing tools that allows new effort to earn real change.

If you're still inside, or fighting for a loved one, here's what you need to remember:

The fight doesn't end at sentencing.

Whether it's a quiet conversation in a holding cell, a document that helps an agent connect the dots, or the courage to finally tell the truth—what you do after that gavel falls can still lead you home.

Stay sharp. Stay strategic.

And never stop learning how to turn the system's own tools into your second chance.

CHAPTER 21

18 U.S.C. § 3582©(1)(A) – Compassionate Release

Part 1: The Door Congress Opened—And You Must Walk Through

There are few moments more final than a federal sentencing hearing. The gavel hits the bench, the judge reads the number, and the marshals lead you away. For many, it feels like the end of the road. But hidden within Title 18 of the United States Code is a powerful truth: your sentence isn't always the end—it can be reconsidered.

That reconsideration lives in 18 U.S.C. § 3582©(1)(A)—better known as compassionate release. Before 2018, this statute was nearly useless. Only the Bureau of Prisons (BOP) could initiate a motion for sentence reduction. If the BOP said no, the court's hands were tied. And the BOP almost always said no. Men and women died behind bars—sick, elderly, alone—not because the judge wouldn't grant release, but because no one was allowed to ask.

Then came the First Step Act of 2018, and with it, a transformation in federal law. Congress rewrote § 3582©(1)(A) to allow incarcerated individuals to file the motion themselves—directly to the judge who sentenced them—if the BOP failed to act within 30 days of a written request.

That one change has led to the early release of thousands. Some had terminal illnesses. Others had lost their children's caregivers. Some were elderly and had already served decades. And others were simply over-sentenced under old laws that have since changed. They all had one thing in common: they found a reason the law calls "extraordinary and compelling," and they put it in front of a judge.

Let's be clear: § 3582©(1)(A) is not easy. Judges deny far more motions than they grant. The standard is high. The process is technical. But the power is real. And if you do it right, you can go home early.

In this chapter, we'll break down everything you need to know to make that happen:

What the law says, and how it changed under the First Step Act

What counts as an "extraordinary and compelling" reason

How courts interpret those reasons

What documents and arguments you need

How to file the motion (with or without a lawyer)

How to respond if the government opposes

What to do if you're denied

And real examples of people who won early release

This isn't theory. It's law. It's hope backed by statute. And if you've been handed too much time, if your circumstances have changed, or if your health, family, or life demands a second look—then this chapter is your blueprint to ask the court to look again.

Part 2: The Law Itself – What § 3582©(1)(A) Really Says and Why It Changed

To use a legal tool effectively, you have to understand its language. You can't just know it exists—you have to know what it says, what it means, and why it was written in the first place. When it comes to § 3582©(1)(A), the history of this statute is just as important as its text. That history explains why you now have power that didn't exist before 2018.

Let's begin with the original version of the law.

Before the First Step Act, § 3582©(1)(A) stated that a federal court could only reduce a sentence if the Director of the Bureau of Prisons filed a motion. This meant the BOP acted as the gatekeeper. A sick prisoner, an elderly inmate, or someone with a family tragedy could not ask the judge directly. They had to rely on the BOP to care enough to act. And the truth was: the BOP almost never acted.

Between 1992 and 2017, the BOP approved less than a few hundred motions nationwide. People died waiting—terminally ill, medically incapacitated, and forgotten. Judges openly criticized the BOP's refusal to act. Congress heard those criticisms.

That's why, when Congress passed the First Step Act of 2018, it rewrote the statute to add one essential sentence:

- "...or upon motion of the defendant after the defendant has fully exhausted all administrative rights to appeal a failure of the Bureau of Prisons to bring a motion...or the lapse of 30 days from the receipt of such a request by the warden of the defendant's facility, whichever is earlier..."

That change gave you, the defendant, the right to file.

Today, the law reads:

- "The court, upon motion of the Director of the Bureau of Prisons, or upon motion of the defendant after the defendant has fully exhausted all administrative rights... may reduce the term of imprisonment... if it finds that extraordinary and compelling reasons warrant such a reduction and that such a reduction is consistent with applicable policy statements issued by the Sentencing Commission."

That's the statute. But courts have clarified what it means—and what it doesn't mean.

The Key Shifts Post–First Step Act

1. You Can File Directly.

You must first submit a written request to your warden asking for compassionate release. If the warden doesn't respond in 30 days, you can go directly to court.

2. The BOP Is No Longer The Gatekeeper.

Their silence or denial no longer stops you. The power to ask now belongs to you.

3. Judges Have Discretion Beyond The Sentencing Commission's Limits.

In United States v. Brooker (Zullo), 976 F.3d 228 (2d Cir. 2020), the Second Circuit held that district courts are not bound by the old policy statements when a defendant files directly. That means the judge—not the Sentencing Commission—gets to decide what's "extraordinary and compelling."

What This Means for You

You no longer have to be terminally ill to qualify.

You don't need the BOP's permission.

You don't have to rely on someone else to act on your behalf.

If you have a valid reason—and you present it well—you now have a real shot at a sentence reduction.

Whether your situation involves medical deterioration, family tragedy, unfair sentencing laws, or evidence of deep personal transformation, § 3582©(1)(A) is the legal bridge between your current sentence and your potential early freedom.

And now that we've covered what the law says and why it changed, let's go deeper.

Part 3: Serious Medical Conditions – When Incarceration Becomes A Death Sentence

One of the most consistently accepted grounds for compassionate release under § 3582©(1)(A) is serious medical deterioration. The logic is simple: federal prison is not a hospital. It's not a hospice. And when someone's health declines to the point where incarceration becomes cruel, dangerous, or medically unsustainable, the law provides a way out.

This category of "extraordinary and compelling reasons" is often the most straightforward—but it still requires strategy, documentation, and precision. The burden is on you to prove that your condition meets the standard and that the Bureau of Prisons is unable or unwilling to provide appropriate care.

Let's break it down.

The Sentencing Commission's Guidance

Although courts are no longer bound by it, U.S.S.G. § 1B1.13, Application Note 1(A) still serves as a reference point. It describes two types of qualifying medical conditions:

1. Terminal Illness –

A serious and advanced illness with an end-of-life trajectory.

This includes:

Metastatic cancer

Advanced ALS

End-stage organ failure

Late-stage dementia

The diagnosis must come from a medical professional and typically includes a prognosis of 18 months or less to live. However, many courts consider compassionate release even when survival is slightly longer, if the deterioration is severe and irreversible.

2. Debilitating Medical Condition –

A serious physical or cognitive condition that substantially diminishes the ability to care for oneself within the environment of a correctional facility.

Examples include:

Paralysis

Stroke aftermath

Severe cardiovascular disease

Diabetes with complications like amputation or blindness

Chronic obstructive pulmonary disease (COPD)

Long COVID or post-viral organ damage

The key question courts ask:

Can this person care for themselves in prison? Can BOP provide sufficient care?

When BOP Medical Care Isn't Enough

The BOP has limited facilities, limited staff, and frequently delayed or denied treatment. Courts have granted release when:

Prisoners miss critical appointments (dialysis, chemo, surgery)

Medical records show delays, misdiagnoses, or declining conditions

The prison environment worsens the condition (e.g., stress-induced strokes, inadequate wheelchair access)

Medications are inconsistent or denied altogether

United States v. Beck, 425 F. Supp. 3d 573 (M.D.N.C. 2019):

In this case, a woman with aggressive breast cancer was denied timely treatment in BOP custody. The court ruled that the BOP's delay in providing care worsened her prognosis, and the condition was clearly "extraordinary and compelling." She was granted compassionate release.

United States v. Wong Chi Fai, 2020 WL 7419800 (S.D.N.Y. Dec. 17, 2020):

An elderly inmate with multiple chronic conditions, including high blood pressure and kidney disease, was granted release due to high risk of COVID-19 complications, even though his sentence was lengthy.

COVID-19 and Health Risk

COVID-19 changed the way courts view health in prison. During the height of the pandemic, thousands of motions were granted for inmates with:

Asthma

Diabetes

Obesity

Heart disease

Immunodeficiency

Even now, post-pandemic, courts continue to consider COVID-19 vulnerability as a factor—especially if it intersects with chronic disease or age. A medical condition that didn't qualify alone may now meet the threshold in combination with documented risks of reinfection or complications.

What You Need to Provide

Your motion must prove your health condition and its impact. That means submitting:

Medical records: recent, detailed, and specific

BOP medical summaries showing missed care or inadequate treatment

Doctor's letters or declarations (preferably from specialists)

Affidavits from family or caregivers confirming support upon release

Evidence of release plan: home, treatment facility, caregiver info

Do not rely solely on general statements like "I have bad health." Courts require proof—lab results, diagnosis reports, treatment logs, and even pictures where appropriate.

Tips for Success

Be specific: Don't just say you're sick. Show how the illness affects your daily function.

Link your condition to your environment: Explain why prison worsens your health.

Emphasize the urgency: Show how delays or lack of care create serious risk.

Humanize your case: Combine the medical data with your rehabilitation story.

Propose a clear plan: Judges are more likely to release someone with housing, treatment, and support arranged.

Bottom Line:

A serious medical condition—especially one worsened by incarceration—is one of the strongest grounds for early release under § 3582©(1)(A). But even serious illness won't get you out unless you document it, explain its impact, and show the court that the BOP is failing to meet your needs. When life is on the line, clarity and evidence matter more than ever.

Part 4: Family Circumstances – When Your Loved Ones Have No One Else

There are few things more painful than being behind bars while your family struggles on the outside. Maybe your mother is aging and sick. Maybe your child's other parent just passed away or became incapacitated. Maybe you were the glue holding your household together, and now everything is falling apart. Under § 3582©(1)(A), those tragic realities can qualify as extraordinary and compelling reasons for a sentence reduction—if you present them the right way.

Family-related motions are some of the most emotional, but they require legal precision. You can't just say your family needs you—you must prove that your release is the only solution to a crisis that can't be resolved without you. Judges don't grant compassionate release just because your child misses you or your spouse is overwhelmed. But if your child's other parent is dead, hospitalized, or mentally unfit—and there is no one else to care for them—you may qualify.

What the Guidelines Say

Although the Sentencing Commission's policy statement isn't binding for defendant-filed motions, most judges still look to it for guidance. U.S.S.G. § 1B1.13, Application Note 1© recognizes two family-related circumstances:

1. Death or incapacitation of the caregiver of the defendant's minor child
2. Incapacitation of the defendant's spouse or registered partner, where the defendant is the only available caregiver

But courts have gone further. Post–First Step Act rulings, especially since United States v. Brooker, have clarified that judges can use their discretion and aren't limited by the narrow definitions of "spouse" or "registered partner." What matters is necessity and lack of alternatives.

Common Scenarios That May Qualify

The parent of your child has died, been incarcerated, or is hospitalized, and there is no one left to provide adequate care.

Your aging or disabled parent was relying on you as a full-time caregiver before your incarceration.

Your spouse or long-term partner is suffering from dementia, a stroke, or advanced illness, and you are the only one capable of providing round-the-clock care.

Your child has special needs, autism, or mental health struggles that require familiarity and stability only you can provide.

Case Law Example: United States v. Wooten, 2020 WL 6119321 (E.D. Ky. Oct. 16, 2020)

The court granted compassionate release to a father whose 16-year-old daughter's mother had died while he was incarcerated. He proved there was no other suitable caregiver, and that he had a concrete plan to care for his daughter upon release. The court ruled that the need to care for his child was "extraordinary and compelling."

Proving Your Family Circumstances Qualify

Your motion must show:

A serious family crisis—not just stress or inconvenience

You are the only available person to resolve it

There are no viable alternatives (no siblings, relatives, social services, or foster care options)

Your release would directly resolve the problem

Supporting documents matter. Include:

Death certificates or hospital records of the other caregiver

Doctor's letters detailing medical conditions

Letters from teachers, counselors, or social workers explaining the child's needs

Affidavits from relatives confirming their inability to take custody or provide care

A release plan showing you have stable housing and are capable of providing care upon release

Avoiding Common Pitfalls

Don't be vague. Simply saying "my child needs me" won't work. Show the full picture.

Don't exaggerate. If there are other adults who can step in, be honest—but explain why they're unfit or unavailable.

Don't assume sympathy is enough. This is a legal motion—not a letter of emotion. Pair your story with evidence.

What If You're the Grandparent or Sibling?

Some courts have granted release to grandparents or siblings who were de facto caregivers—especially when the alternative is foster care or institutionalization. Again, the key is necessity. Show that you were the primary caregiver and that there is no one else.

Why This Category Matters

This ground for compassionate release touches on something that every judge understands: family responsibility. If you can prove that your absence is putting a child or vulnerable adult at risk—and your presence would resolve it—judges are willing to listen.

But you have to bring your case with strength, structure, and undeniable documentation.

Part 5: Age And Time Served – When Enough Time Really Is Enough

Time can break a person down in federal prison. The body ages faster. The mind wears thinner. Years that might've been rehabilitative for someone younger become oppressive, even dangerous, for someone older. That's why another critical path to compassionate release under 18 U.S.C. § 3582©(1)(A) is based on a combination of age and time served. The argument is simple: I've done enough. My risk to society is gone. My continued incarceration serves no purpose.

In the eyes of the court, aging out of criminal behavior is real. Statistically, the older you get, the less likely you are to reoffend. And judges know this. So, if you're in your 60s or older—and you've served a significant chunk of your sentence—you may qualify for early release, even if your case doesn't involve medical issues or a family emergency.

What the Guidelines Say (Even Though They're Not Binding)

The old policy statement from the Sentencing Commission—U.S.S.G. § 1B1.13, Application Note 1(B)—offered some guidance for BOP-initiated motions, saying that a reduction could be considered when:

- "The defendant (i) is at least 65 years old; (ii) is experiencing a serious deterioration in physical or mental health because of the aging process; and (iii) has served at least 10 years or 75 percent of the term of imprisonment, whichever is less."
- That's a useful benchmark. But since the First Step Act, courts are no longer bound by this. Many judges have now granted compassionate release to people who don't fit that exact mold—but who are elderly, rehabilitated, and over-sentenced.

Case Law Example: United States v. Millan, 2020 WL 1674058 (S.D.N.Y. Apr. 6, 2020)

Mr. Millan was sentenced to life in prison for drug trafficking. He was in his 60s and had already served 28 years. He had no disciplinary issues and had shown extraordinary rehabilitation. The court granted his motion, finding that his age, time served, clean prison record, and low risk of recidivism justified early release.

Judge Analisa Torres wrote:

- "Mr. Millan has demonstrated that he is not the man he was when he was sentenced... and that continued incarceration is no longer necessary to protect the public or provide just punishment."

This is exactly the kind of thinking that § 3582©(1)(A) was meant to encourage.

Key Factors That Strengthen Age-Based Motions

You are 60 or older

You've served 10 years or more, or a significant portion of your sentence

You have minimal or no disciplinary record

You've completed programming, earned GEDs, taught or mentored others

You have a clean release plan and stable support system

You're not a physical threat due to age, health, or nature of conviction

Even if you don't have a medical diagnosis, advanced age alone, especially in combination with strong rehabilitation, can tip the scales in your favor.

COVID-19 Amplified These Arguments

Many courts recognized that older age plus incarceration during a pandemic creates an even more compelling case for release. Judges began to view advanced age as a risk multiplier—not just a marker of maturity.

What You Need to Present

Your current age and projected release date

Your prison history (programs completed, work record, incident-free record)

Letters of support from family or community members

Release plan with housing, medical care (if needed), and transportation

Statistics or expert reports on recidivism and aging

For example, quote DOJ or Sentencing Commission studies showing dramatically reduced reoffense rates for those over 60

Judicial Language You Should Echo in Your Motion

When writing or dictating your motion, use the words "extraordinary and compelling", but also include terms like:

"no longer a threat to the community"

"rehabilitated beyond what was expected"

"continued incarceration serves no meaningful purpose"

"this sentence no longer reflects the goals of § 3553(a)"

"incarceration beyond this point becomes punitive, not corrective"

Bottom Line

If you are growing old in prison, and you've served a serious portion of your sentence, the law gives your judge the power to look again. Courts across the country are starting to agree that a long sentence served well is not wasted time—but it doesn't need to be a life sentence, either.

You've paid a debt. And in some cases, that payment has been more than enough.

Part 6: Sentencing Disparities And Unjust Laws – When The Rules Have Changed But Your Sentence Hasn't

There may be no pain quite like watching the law change after you've already been buried by it. Men and women sentenced to 40, 50, or even life in prison—now seeing others convicted of the same crime walk away with half the time or less. It happens more than most people realize. And while Congress doesn't always make new laws retroactive, compassionate release under § 3582©(1)(A) has become a lifeline for people trapped under old rules.

If the law has changed, and your sentence no longer reflects the values of justice or proportionality, you have an argument—a powerful one—for why your continued incarceration is "extraordinary and compelling."

Understanding This Ground for Compassionate Release

Sentencing disparity-based motions often arise in cases where:

The statute has changed (e.g., stacking of § 924© firearm offenses)

The Sentencing Guidelines have been lowered, but not made retroactive

The First Step Act reduced penalties for crack cocaine—but you were sentenced under the old 100:1 ratio

You were sentenced as a "career offender" under criteria that courts or science now reject

Codefendants or co-conspirators received far less time than you—often due to cooperation

This is your opportunity to argue that justice evolved—but your sentence didn't.

Case Law: United States v. McCoy, 981 F.3d 271 (4th Cir. 2020)

The court granted compassionate release to several men who were serving stacked mandatory sentences under 18 U.S.C. § 924©—a harsh practice that required 25 years for a second firearm count, even in a first-time case. Congress changed the rule under the First Step Act, but didn't make it retroactive.

The court wrote:

- "The district courts permissibly treated as 'extraordinary and compelling reasons' the severity of the defendants' § 924© sentences and the extent of the disparity between the defendants' sentences and those provided for under the First Step Act."

McCoy opened the door for judges to say: Even if Congress didn't make the change retroactive—we can still acknowledge that it would be wrong to ignore it.

Other Powerful Examples

Crack vs. Powder Cocaine: If you were sentenced under the 100:1 ratio and didn't benefit from the Fair Sentencing Act or First Step Act, you may now qualify.

Career Offender Redefinition: Some old convictions once classified as "crimes of violence" no longer qualify. That changes everything.

Parole-eligible inmates stuck on mandatory minimums: Especially in DC and older federal sentences.

Drastic sentencing differences between co-defendants: If your codefendant received a significant reduction—especially if it was post-First Step Act or post-plea—you may have grounds.

What You Need to Argue

This isn't about bitterness. It's about fairness. You must show:

1. The law has changed—either by statute or through case law
2. You would receive a significantly lower sentence if sentenced today
3. You've served a substantial amount of time already
4. You have demonstrated rehabilitation
5. Your continued incarceration would be unjust in light of new norms
6. The § 3553(a) factors now support release

How To Build The Motion

Attach your original judgment and sentencing memorandum

Explain clearly how the law has changed (cite case law or statute)

Provide comparisons (e.g., same offense now receives 10 years less)

Include rehabilitation records, program completions, and good behavior

Emphasize your release plan and low risk of recidivism

Reference prior rulings like McCoy, Brooker, or Arellano to show precedent

Ask the court to acknowledge the disparity and use its discretion

What Judges Look For

Judges are more likely to grant release under this category when:

The original sentence is disproportionately harsh

The change in law is widely acknowledged as corrective

The defendant has served 15+ years or a majority of the time

The defendant shows genuine reform, not just compliance

There is a strong release plan, support system, and no risk to public safety

Judicial Quotes to Use in Your Motion

- "The sentence now serves no rehabilitative, deterrent, or retributive purpose."

"To ignore the evolution of justice would be to endorse an injustice."

"Congress chose not to make this law retroactive—but § 3582 gives this court the authority to correct its moral consequence."

Bottom Line

If the law has moved forward—but your sentence is still frozen in the past—you have a voice, and the court has the power to listen. § 3582©(1)(A) was written for cases like yours. Where the structure of the law has changed, but its shadow still remains.

Part 7: Rehabilitation – When Change Behind Bars Becomes Your Freedom Argument

Some people never change in prison. Others change on paper—just enough to impress the parole board or the case manager. But then there are the few who change for real.

They don't just behave—they evolve. They read everything they can get their hands on. They lead others. They educate, mentor, and rebuild from within. They do the work—without promise, without fanfare, and often without hope. For those individuals, rehabilitation itself can be the reason a judge sends them home early.

While rehabilitation alone is not enough under § 3582©(1)(A)—and Congress explicitly said so—courts are now increasingly recognizing that exceptional rehabilitation is often what tips the balance in close calls. When paired with other factors—like age, sentencing disparity, or even time served—your growth can be the difference between a denial and your freedom.

What the Law Says—and What Courts Are Now Doing

In 28 U.S.C. § 994(t), Congress directed the Sentencing Commission that:

- "Rehabilitation of the defendant alone shall not be considered an extraordinary and compelling reason."

But this doesn't mean that rehabilitation doesn't matter. In fact, in most compassionate release grants, the court spends significant time discussing how the defendant has changed. Why? Because § 3582©(1)(A) still requires the judge to evaluate the sentencing factors under § 3553(a)—including:

The history and characteristics of the defendant

The need to protect the public

The need for rehabilitation

Whether continued incarceration promotes respect for the law

So while you can't walk into court and say, "I changed, now let me out," you can say, "I've changed—and given everything else, keeping me in prison no longer makes sense."

Case Law Example: United States v. Millan, 2020 WL 1674058 (S.D.N.Y. Apr. 6, 2020)

Mr. Millan had served 28 years of a life sentence. He was a model prisoner who mentored others, earned educational credits, and made peace with the harm he had caused. He had no major medical issues and wasn't relying on law changes to support his release. Still, the judge reduced his sentence to time served, writing:

- "Mr. Millan has shown extraordinary rehabilitation... and continued incarceration would serve no useful purpose."

What Exceptional Rehabilitation Looks Like

Program completion: GED, college courses, vocational programs, RDAP

Leadership: Facilitating classes, mentoring younger inmates, creating reentry programs

Employment history: Long-term UNICOR work, job training, spotless institutional record

Zero disciplinary infractions, or minimal and distant in time

Letters of support: From counselors, staff, teachers, family, and fellow inmates

Personal transformation: Faith, therapy, written self-reflection, purpose

Giving back: Volunteering, peer tutoring, parenting classes, restorative justice efforts

This isn't about perfection. It's about proof of change—not just compliance, but growth.

Documents to Include in a Rehabilitation-Based Motion

BOP Program Achievement Reports

Certificates of completion

Work performance reviews from supervisors

Personal letters from chaplains, psychologists, and correctional staff

Essays, coursework, or writing that shows self-reflection and accountability

Affidavits from cellmates or mentees who've benefited from your guidance

Photos or video (if possible) from programs you led

Your release plan: job offer, housing, community support, parole plan (if required)

Strategic Phrases to Use in the Motion

- "This individual has outgrown the behavior that led to incarceration."

"The goals of punishment have already been met."

"There is nothing left for prison to teach him/her."

"A sentence meant to break has instead built a better person."

"Any further incarceration is punitive, not corrective."

When Rehabilitation Becomes the Tipping Point

Rehabilitation is especially powerful when:

The original sentence was harsh, but not unlawful

The motion is borderline—like minor medical issues or family crises that need extra weight

The individual has served 10+ years

You have no new disciplinary infractions in the past 5+ years

You've built a detailed reentry plan with housing, employment, and supervision

In these cases, rehabilitation doesn't need to be the only reason—it just needs to be the final reason.

Bottom Line:

No judge wants to release someone just because they say they've changed. But if you show that you've rebuilt yourself from the inside out—and you pair that growth with a compelling legal argument—the court may agree that your time has been served, your sentence has done its job, and you've earned your way back home.

Part 8: How To Write And File Your Own Compassionate Release Motion

A Step-by-Step Guide for Doing It Without a Lawyer

When you're on the inside, time moves differently. You may not have access to a lawyer. You may not have money for one. But what you do have is the right to file for your own release. 18 U.S.C. § 3582©(1)(A) gives you that power. And in this section, you'll learn how to use it—step by step, even if you're filing pro se (representing yourself).

Don't worry about sounding like a lawyer. Focus on truth, structure, and evidence. Many pro se inmates have successfully filed and won these motions because they followed the process, documented their claims, and made their humanity known to the court.

Let's walk through the full motion process.

Step 1: Exhaust Your Administrative Remedy – Write to the Warden

Before you can file in court, you must first ask your warden in writing for compassionate release. This is called "exhausting administrative remedies." The law requires it.

Your request should include:

Your name, register number, and facility

A short explanation of the reason you believe you qualify (medical condition, family emergency, change in law, etc.)

A specific request for "the BOP or Warden to file a motion for compassionate release under 18 U.S.C. § 3582©(1)(A)"

Keep a copy of this request. If they deny it or don't respond within 30 days, you're allowed to file directly with the court.

Step 2: Prepare Your Motion for the Court

Your motion doesn't need to be perfect. But it does need to be clear, truthful, and supported by documentation.

Title your motion something like:

- Motion for Sentence Reduction Pursuant to 18 U.S.C. § 3582©(1)(A)

Your motion should include these key sections:

A. Introduction

Example:

- Comes now, [Your Full Name], pro se, respectfully requesting that this Honorable Court reduce my sentence under 18 U.S.C. § 3582©(1)(A) due to extraordinary and compelling reasons, and in support, I state the following:

B. Background of Your Case

Briefly explain:

Your original sentence

The charge(s) you were convicted of

How long you've served

Any key factors at sentencing (e.g., judge's remarks, 924© stacking, lack of criminal history)

C. Grounds for Relief

Now explain the reason you're asking for compassionate release. This could be:

A serious medical condition

The death/incapacitation of a caregiver

A dramatic change in the law that affects your sentence

Advanced age and time served

Exceptional rehabilitation

A combination of the above

Use your own words. But be direct. Example:

- I am 65 years old and have served 22 years. I suffer from congestive heart failure and have required emergency hospitalization twice in the past year. The prison lacks adequate facilities to treat my condition, and my health is deteriorating rapidly.

D. Application of § 3553(a) Sentencing Factors

Tell the court that:

You are no longer a danger to society

You've completed programs, stayed discipline-free, helped others

You have a release plan (housing, job, community support)

Continued incarceration does not promote justice, deterrence, or rehabilitation

Example:

- The goals of sentencing have been served. I have worked in UNICOR, earned my GED, completed RDAP, and mentored others. I am no longer the same man I wa

  when I entered prison, and I respectfully ask this Court to weigh these factors in granting relief.

E. Relief Requested

Be specific. Example:

- I respectfully ask the Court to reduce my sentence to time served and to order immediate release, or in the alternative, to modify my sentence to home confinement or supervised release.

Step 3: Attach Supporting Documents

Include:

Medical records

Program certificates

Incident-free record printout

Letters of support (family, mentors, community leaders)

Release plan (address, medical follow-up, job if applicable)

Copy of the request you sent to the warden

Any legal citations that support your case

Step 4: File Your Motion With the Court

Address it to the same judge who sentenced you, at the U.S. District Court where your case was handled.

Use this format:

> Clerk of Court

U.S. District Court for the [District Name]

[Address]

Re: United States v. [Your Name], Case No. [Your Original Case Number]

Motion for Compassionate Release Pursuant to 18 U.S.C. § 3582©(1)(A)

Send it by certified mail if possible, and keep a copy of everything.

Step 5: Wait for the Court's Response

The court may assign your motion to the judge and order the government to respond.

In some cases, the court may appoint a public defender to help.

You may or may not be granted a hearing—many rulings are made based on the paperwork.

Be patient—but stay in communication with anyone assisting you on the outside.

Final Tip: Keep a Copy of Everything

The court can only consider what it sees. If your health worsens, your family situation changes, or you complete more programs, you can file a second motion or update the court with a supplemental filing.

Part 9: If The Court Says No – What To Do After A Denial And How To Stay Ready

Even with a strong motion, powerful documents, and a compelling reason, the court might still say no. Compassionate release is discretionary, not guaranteed. Judges are cautious. Some districts are more conservative. And sometimes, timing just isn't right.

But here's the truth:

A denial does not mean it's over.

It means not yet.

And in federal court, persistence—done strategically—can be the difference between serving 20 years and walking out in 12.

This section is about what to do after a denial and how to keep yourself positioned for another shot.

1. Understand the Judge's Reasoning

Start with the order denying your motion. Courts usually explain their reasoning in writing. It might include:

"Extraordinary and compelling reasons not demonstrated"

"§ 3553(a) factors still weigh against release"

"Danger to the community"

"Not enough time served"

"No release plan provided"

"Rehabilitation alone is insufficient"

Read that reasoning carefully. It tells you what needs to change next time.

If the denial was because of missing documentation, lack of medical evidence, or incomplete filing, those things are fixable. If it was about not enough time served, you may simply need to wait another year and file again with new facts.

2. You Can File Again—If Your Circumstances Change

A compassionate release denial is not a "with prejudice" judgment unless the judge specifically says so. That means:

If your health worsens

If your family situation changes (e.g., caregiver dies, child's situation deteriorates)

If you complete more rehabilitation programs

If laws evolve or co-defendants get released

If you secure housing, job offers, or support letters

You can file again.

Example: If your first motion failed because of limited medical evidence, and you're later diagnosed with a worsening condition, gather the records and submit a new motion under § 3582©(1)(A) based on "new extraordinary and compelling circumstances."

3. Supplement Your Prior Motion if the Judge Leaves the Door Open

Sometimes, the court won't deny outright—but will say something like:

- "At this time, the motion is denied without prejudice. The Court may reconsider upon presentation of updated medical records or further documentation."

That is a signal.

It means: Get your paperwork right, and come back.

File a motion to supplement the record, or if time has passed, file a new § 3582 motion with updated evidence and explain briefly what has changed.

4. Appeal (Cautiously)

You have the right to appeal a denial of compassionate release to the U.S. Court of Appeals. But be careful: most appeals are denied unless the judge clearly misapplied the law.

If you want to appeal:

Do it within 14 days of the ruling

Only appeal if there is a legal mistake—not just because you disagree

Use the appeal to preserve your issue for future retroactive application (like if the Sentencing Commission expands eligibility criteria)

For most people, filing a stronger second motion is more effective than appealing a first denial.

5. Keep Building Your Case Every Day

A denial should trigger one response: get stronger.

Enroll in more programming

Earn certifications or degrees

Mentor others

Build community ties (letters, job plans, therapy referrals)

Stay discipline-free

Get updated medical checkups

Educate yourself on new case law or changes in the Sentencing Commission's rules

Prepare a better release plan (housing, job, support network)

Then update the court when something major changes—especially if the judge left the record open for it.

6. Stay Informed on Changing Laws and Amendments

The Sentencing Commission regularly updates its policy statements. A proposed amendment in 2023 added more scenarios to "extraordinary and compelling reasons," including:

Being a caregiver

Victim of abuse by corrections officers

Lengthy sentences under laws that are now outdated

Youth at the time of offense

Stay ready. The law is alive, and if it changes in your favor, you need to be first in line with a new motion.

7. Ask the Court to Appoint Counsel If You File Again

Many courts will appoint a federal public defender once you file a strong, legally sound motion. In your next motion, you can include a line at the end:

- "Defendant respectfully requests the appointment of counsel pursuant to 18 U.S.C. § 3006A should the Court find further briefing or representation appropriate."

This increases your chance of having help to fine-tune the arguments and respond to the government.

Bottom Line

A "no" isn't failure. It's feedback.

Every denial is a map of what to fix, prove, or present better. You're still in the fight. You still have the law on your side. And the court still has the power to grant your release.

Your job is to stay ready. Stay righteous. And stay writing.

SUMMARY

Part 1 Summary

Part 1 lays the groundwork for understanding the critical legal factors that can pave the way for a downward departure in sentencing. It begins with the powerful idea that cooperation with authorities can become a lifeline, offering a chance for a reduced sentence in exchange for a willingness to assist law enforcement. This chapter also highlights the role criminal history plays, with an acknowledgment that a defendant's past should not automatically define their future. The discussion of mental capacity paints a picture of how the law recognizes the complexities of the human mind—how a person's mental state can influence their level of culpability and, in turn, their punishment. Furthermore, the chapter underscores the transformative potential of post-offense rehabilitation, illustrating how genuine change after committing a crime can be seen as a step toward redemption. The emotional core of this part revolves around the potential for growth and transformation, emphasizing that one's past doesn't have to dictate their future, and how the justice system can recognize efforts to evolve.

Part 2 Summary

Part 2 shifts focus to the deeply personal and human elements that can influence sentencing. It explores the critical role that family obligations play, showing how the impact of a sentence on a defendant's loved ones can be a powerful factor in mitigating punishment. Age is also examined, reminding us that the context of one's life—whether young or old—can significantly affect the appropriateness of a harsh sentence. Central to this part is the theme of personal responsibility, the emotional weight that comes with acknowledging one's wrongdoings, and the profound power of showing genuine remorse. The defendant's role in the crime is also scrutinized—whether they were a mere participant or a driving force behind the offense. In this part, there is a palpable sense of hope, highlighting how human connections and personal growth can shape a path toward a more lenient sentence. There's an understanding that individuals are more than their crimes, and the emotional toll of making amends and taking responsibility can be life-altering.

Part 3 Summary

Part 3 delves into the external factors that can weigh heavily on a defendant's sentence. It brings to light how debilitating health conditions—physical or mental—can drastically alter the course of one's life, affecting not only their physical well-being but their ability to serve a sentence. Coercion and duress are explored in depth, with an understanding that sometimes individuals find themselves in situations where their freedom or safety is at risk, forcing them into actions they never would have chosen otherwise. In this part, the victim's conduct is discussed, providing a nuanced perspective on how the actions of others can create or exacerbate the circumstances leading to the crime. The involvement of others, too, is considered, as it speaks to the complexity of human actions and interactions—how a single person's involvement may have been minimal, or they may have been swept up by a greater force at play. Part 3 is deeply empathetic, recognizing that outside pressures, health struggles, and manipulation can sometimes shape an individual's fate in ways they never anticipated. The emotional depth of this section lies in its acknowledgment of human vulnerability and how external circumstances can sometimes strip away a person's agency, making them more than just the crime they committed.

Part 4 Summary

Safety Valve Recap: A Second Chance Hidden in the Law

Bringing It All Together

The safety valve is more than a legal tool—it's a lifeline. For nonviolent federal defendants facing mandatory minimums, it can be the single most important path to reclaiming time, freedom, and the possibility of returning home sooner to rebuild. But relief under 18 U.S.C. § 3553(f) is not automatic. It must be earned, proven, and navigated carefully.

You must meet all five requirements. Miss one, and the valve closes.

In Part 1, we explored the foundation: the safety valve exists to give low-level, nonviolent offenders a break from unjustly long mandatory sentences. It is meant for those who have made mistakes—but who do not pose a long-term threat to society and who take responsibility for their actions.

Part 2 addressed criminal history. The math matters. You must have no more than four criminal history points (excluding 1-point offenses), and no disqualifying violent or drug trafficking priors. Even a single 3-point violent conviction can block you. This step demands a detailed review of your record—and sometimes, a fight over how your past is being calculated.

Part 3 centered on violence, threats, and firearms. If a weapon was used, possessed, or even nearby during the crime—or if any threats were made—you may be disqualified. It doesn't matter whether the gun was fired or whether the violence was planned. What matters is whether your offense was connected to force, danger, or intimidation.

In Part 4, we covered the third condition: no death or serious bodily injury can result from the offense. Even if the injury was unintended or caused by someone else, if it flowed directly from the offense, the safety valve may be off-limits. Courts look for causation, impact, and proximity to harm.

Part 5 tackled the question of leadership. If you were an organizer, manager, or supervisor in any part of the offense, you lose eligibility. But if you were a courier, assistant, or minor player—someone who didn't give orders or control others—you may still qualify. Understanding your role, and how the law views it, is key.

And finally, Part 6 discussed truthfulness. This requirement is not about cooperation. It's about accountability. You must tell the full truth about your actions and related conduct before sentencing. This debrief must be complete, honest, and timely. The usefulness of the information doesn't matter—only that it's truthful.

Together, these five elements form a tight gate. But for those who pass through, the reward can be life-altering. Avoiding a 5, 10, or 20-year mandatory minimum sentence gives a person the chance to start over sooner—to raise their children, care for loved ones, or simply live with hope again.

The safety valve Is not mercy for the guilty—it's justice for those whose conduct, circumstances, and character show they deserve more than a one-size-fits-all punishment.

If you qualify, fight for it.

If you're unsure, investigate it.

And if you're disqualified now, stay focused—because laws evolve, and second chances have a way of finding the prepared.

Your freedom may depend on understanding this provision better than anyone else in the room. Use it wisely.

Part 5 Summary

Rule 35 of the Federal Rules of Criminal Procedure provides one of the few legal pathways to reduce a federal sentence after it's been imposed. It operates in two parts:

1. Rule 35(b) – Substantial Assistance Reductions

35(b)(1): Allows the government to request a sentence reduction within one year of sentencing if the defendant provides substantial assistance in investigating or prosecuting others. This includes testifying, supplying credible evidence, or helping dismantle criminal networks.

35(b)(2): Applies after one year, but only if:

A) the defendant learns new information post-sentencing,

B) early-provided info becomes useful later, or

C) the value of info wasn't apparent until after one year.

In both, only the government can file the motion. If filed, the judge can reduce the sentence to any length, even time served.

2. Rule 35(a) – Correcting Clear Errors

Allows the court to correct a sentence within 14 days if it contains a clear error, such as a mathematical mistake or misapplication of the law. This is a narrow rule and cannot be used to challenge legal discretion or raise new arguments.

Bottom Line:

Rule 35 is a powerful but limited tool. For those willing to assist the government after sentencing, it can lead to significant sentence reductions. For those facing a sentencing mistake, it offers a brief window for correction. It's not a right—it's a door that opens only through credibility, timing, and strategic legal support.

Part 6 Summary

In a system where long sentences feel permanent and justice often moves too slowly, 18 U.S.C. § 3582©(1)(A) is a powerful exception. It's not mercy—it's law. It's a hard-earned second chance backed by statute and sharpened by the First Step Act. If you're still reading this, you're not just hoping for that chance—you're preparing to take it.

You now understand what many people behind bars do not:

That you don't need the Bureau of Prisons to speak for you anymore.

That a judge can reexamine your sentence when real-life circumstances change.

That "extraordinary and compelling" is not a myth—it's a legal standard, with pathways carved by illness, family crisis, age, unjust laws, and transformation.

You've learned:

How to exhaust your remedies by writing to the warden

How to build and structure a motion with clarity, truth, and documentation

What kinds of evidence matter—from medical records to rehabilitation history

How to use changes in law or sentencing disparities as your foundation

Why a strong release plan is just as important as your reason for release

How to handle a denial, adapt, and come back stronger

What courts are looking for: responsibility, readiness, and purpose

More importantly, you've been told what no lawyer, no counselor, and no jailhouse rumor might ever make clear:

- You are not powerless.

You are not forgotten.

You are not without tools to fight for your own freedom.

Whether you're sick, aging, the last hope for your child, or simply someone who's done the time and become a better person—this law gives you the right to ask for release. And if your motion is honest, grounded, and thorough, the judge has the power to say yes.

So don't wait for someone else to write it for you.

Don't leave it to chance.

And don't let silence speak for you.

Write your motion.

File it.

Document your change.

Prove your worth.

Because this law wasn't written for perfect people—it was written for people who've paid enough, learned enough, and are ready to go home.

And that might be you.

Practical Tips for Building Your Case

When seeking a downward departure, it's essential to build a compelling case that highlights the factors that could reduce the severity of your sentence. Here are some practical steps you can take:

1. Gather Supporting Documentation: To present your case effectively, you'll need solid evidence. Whether it's proof of family obligations, records of post-offense rehabilitation, or medical documents for health conditions, be sure to collect any relevant paperwork that supports your claim. The more specific and detailed the documentation, the stronger your case will be.

2. Show Genuine Remorse: Demonstrating that you understand the consequences of your actions and have taken responsibility is crucial. Writing a personal letter to the judge expressing your remorse and detailing what steps you've taken to change can be powerful. Include specific examples of how you've worked on yourself, whether through therapy, education, or community service.

3. Work on Your Rehabilitation: If you're arguing for a reduction based on post-offense rehabilitation or diminished capacity, show that you've made tangible progress. Complete any educational or vocational programs, attend therapy, or participate in volunteer work. These actions demonstrate that you are committed to bettering yourself and are taking responsibility for your past behavior.

4. Highlight Your Personal Circumstances: Family obligations or age can be strong mitigating factors. Provide evidence of your role as a caregiver, parent, or support system for someone who depends on you. Similarly, if you're young or elderly, focus on how your age and potential for rehabilitation should be taken into account. Document any hardships your family or community may face without you.

5. Work with Your Attorney: Your legal team can help you present these factors in the best light possible. Be open and honest with them about the circumstances surrounding your case and work together to find the most effective strategy for seeking a downward departure.

The Role of Legal Counsel

Legal counsel plays a pivotal role in your downward departure request. While you may be familiar with your own life circumstances and the factors that could lead to a reduced sentence, an attorney brings the legal expertise needed to navigate the complexities of the court system.

1. Strategic Case Building: Your attorney can help identify which factors—whether it's your role in the offense, family obligations, health issues, or rehabilitation—are most likely to lead to a successful downward departure request. They can also help you gather the right evidence and present it in the most persuasive way.

2. Legal Knowledge and Experience: Understanding the intricacies of federal sentencing guidelines and case law is essential. A knowledgeable attorney will be able to argue your case within the framework of the law, ensuring that all relevant rules and precedents are considered in your favor.

3. Filing the Motion: An attorney will ensure that all necessary paperwork is filed properly and on time. They will also handle any motions or hearings that need to take place, ensuring that you have the best chance for a reduced sentence.

4. Negotiating with the Prosecution: In many cases, your attorney can work with the prosecution to negotiate a plea deal or a favorable recommendation for a downward departure. Their ability to communicate with the prosecution and advocate on your behalf is a crucial part of the process.

5. Emotional Support and Guidance: Going through this process can be overwhelming, and your attorney can provide not just legal support but emotional guidance as well. They'll help you stay focused on your goal and manage the stress that comes with navigating the legal system.

Potential Challenges and Pitfalls

While seeking a downward departure can significantly reduce your sentence, there are challenges and potential obstacles that may arise during the process. Here are some common pitfalls to watch out for:

1. Overcoming Skepticism: Judges may be skeptical of claims for a downward departure, especially if the evidence is weak or the circumstances aren't clear. For example, arguing that the victim's conduct contributed to the crime might be met with resistance unless there's strong evidence to support the claim.

2. Failure to Provide Sufficient Evidence: Without clear and convincing documentation—such as medical records, proof of rehabilitation, or family affidavits—the court may be less inclined to consider a downward departure. Make sure all evidence is thorough, organized, and up-to-date.

3. Inconsistent or Lack of Remorse: If you've not demonstrated genuine remorse or accepted responsibility for your actions, a judge may not take your request seriously. It's important that you show accountability, not just through words but through actions like rehabilitation or personal development programs.

4. Limited Applicability of Certain Factors: Not all downward departure factors may apply to your case. For instance, arguments based on age or a minor role in the offense may not be persuasive if your involvement was significant or if you're not eligible for those specific considerations. Be realistic about which factors can actually work in your favor.

5. Legal Representation: If you have ineffective legal counsel or if your attorney is unable to present your case in the strongest possible light, it could reduce your chances of success. Make sure you have an attorney who is experienced in sentencing hearings and who is willing to fight for a reduction in your sentence.

What You Say Can Haunt You – Surviving the Change of Plea Hearing

The courtroom can feel like a trap wrapped in formality. The judge's voice is calm. Your lawyer nudges you to answer "yes" or "no." You're told it's just procedure. Just a formality. Just a change of plea hearing. But let me tell you the truth: this is not just a formality—it's a minefield. And what you say here can come back to haunt you in ways you won't understand until it's too late.

During the plea colloquy, the judge will ask you a series of questions. Some of them feel harmless. Some might even seem like they're meant to help. But each one is a trapdoor if you're not careful—especially if you ever plan to file a § 2255 motion claiming ineffective assistance of counsel. Because once you say it on the record, they will hold you to it like scripture.

One of the most dangerous questions the judge will ask is:

"Are you satisfied with your attorney's performance?"

And in that moment—nervous, rushed, trusting the system—you may want to say yes.

Don't.

If you say, "Yes, he did a good job," that one sentence will be used against you later, even if your lawyer never filed a motion, never investigated your case, never went over the PSR, or even pressured you into pleading guilty without a defense. That one sentence becomes the judge's shield. When you later try to explain how your attorney failed you, the judge will say:

- "But you told me under oath that you were satisfied."

Here's what you should say, respectfully, clearly, and on the record:

- "With all due respect, Your Honor, I cannot answer that question at this time. We have not gone over the Presentence Investigation Report, nor have we had the sentencing hearing. I don't yet know how he will perform during those stages, which are critical. I reserve my right to evaluate counsel's performance after all proceedings are complete."

You have that right. Don't let anyone silence you.

And when the judge asks if anyone made you promises to get you to plead guilty—tell the truth.

If your lawyer, the prosecutor, or anyone else promised you a lower sentence, a program, or told you the judge would "go easy"—say it. Get it on the record. If they say they didn't promise anything, but you remember otherwise, speak up. Do not stay silent just to move things along or avoid confrontation.

Also, if the judge asks, "Is this plea voluntary?"—but your lawyer pressured you, threatened to withdraw, or didn't explain the plea fully—do not say yes. Say what actually happened. Speak your truth. Because if you don't, your silence will become their weapon.

Understand this: the change of plea hearing is only the first of three critical stages. After this, you'll go through the PSR (Presentence Report) interview, which determines the sentencing range the judge will use. Then you'll face the sentencing hearing itself. If your lawyer hasn't prepared, challenged the drug amounts, argued against enhancements, or addressed restitution or forfeiture—you won't know that yet during the plea. So why would you give them a clean bill of health?

Don't lie. But don't trap yourself, either.

Speak carefully. Speak truthfully. And speak for yourself.

This is your life.

Your time.

Your record.

And when it's all said and done, it's your voice the record will hold. Make sure it tells the truth.

Closing Call To Action

Your future is in your hands, and understanding the options available to you is the first step toward a brighter tomorrow. A downward departure is not just a legal term—it's a chance for a second chance, a chance to rebuild your life, and a chance to return home to the people who need you most.

Whether you are motivated by family, a desire for personal redemption, or the opportunity to make a meaningful change in your life, you have the power to make your case. With the right documentation, support, and legal counsel, you can advocate for a sentence that reflects not just your crime, but the person you are today and the person you aim to become.

Take control of your story. Fight for the opportunity to go home, to be with your family, to heal, and to continue your journey toward a positive future. Start building your case today, and never forget that the possibility of redemption is always within reach.

About The Author

Patrick Hall Sr. is a federal prisoner who was sentenced to 23 years in the United States criminal justice system. But instead of letting time break him, he used it to build purpose. While incarcerated, Patrick dedicated himself to studying the law, mastering sentencing reform statutes, and becoming a powerful voice for those who've been silenced by excessive prison terms and unequal justice.

Driven by his own experience—and by the stories of men around him who lacked resources, education, or legal support—Patrick committed his life to fighting for fairness, especially when it comes to sentencing disparities that overwhelmingly affect the poor, minorities, and the voiceless.

From behind prison walls, he became a student, a legal researcher, and a strategist—spending thousands of hours learning how to challenge injustice through the system that once buried him. His passion is rooted in one belief: everyone deserves a second chance when they've shown accountability, change, and the will to return better than they came.

Through his writing, Patrick Hall Sr. hopes to empower others with the tools he had to find on his own—the tools that can open the doors to freedom, family, and a new beginning. This book is a product of that mission.

"I wrote this because somebody has to tell the truth about what hope looks like in a system designed to erase it."

—Patrick Hall Sr.

OTHER BOOKS PUBLISHED BY P. HALL PUBLISHING AND ENTERTAINMENT LLC

(Available On Amazon & Barnes and noble)

www.ingramcontent.com/pod-product-compliance
Lightning Source LLC
LaVergne TN
LVHW082347200926
848481LV00012B/3484